AE

THE HISTORY OF PORT CHATHAM, ALASKA

By
Larry Baxter

www.alasquatchpodcast.com

ABANDONED
The History and Horror of Port Chatham, Alaska

Copyright © 2021 by Larry A. Baxter

All rights reserved. No part of this publication may be reproduced, stored in a retrieval system, or transmitted in any form or by any means, electronic, mechanical, photocopying, recording, scanning, or otherwise, without prior permission in writing from the copyright owner.

ISBN: 978-1-7367297-0-0 (Paperback)
ISBN: 978-1-7367297-1-7 (E-book)

Library of Congress Control Number: 2021903659

Published by Larry A. Baxter
Edited by Tammaron K. Baxter

Cover Photo Courtesy of Extreme Expeditions Northwest, LLC
Cover Design by Larry A. Baxter

Alasquatch Publishing
PO Box 887
Homer, Alaska 99603

www.alasquatchpodcast.com

Dedication

This work is dedicated to my wife, Tammaron, who supports me in all of my endeavors and has spent many nights lying awake, wondering if I was going to make it home. It is also dedicated to those who are brave enough to seek the truth, and especially to those strong enough to tell it.

CHAPTER 1 THINGS THAT GO BUMP IN THE WOODS 1

CHAPTER 2 THE GREAT SASQUATCH HUNTER 8

CHAPTER 3 ALASKA'S PLAYGROUND 12

CHAPTER 4 PORT CHATHAM, ALASKA 1931 16

CHAPTER 5 A TREASURE TROVE OF NATURAL RESOURCES 26

CHAPTER 6 THE NANTIINAQ 31

CHAPTER 7 THE PROSPECTOR 40

CHAPTER 8 THE VICTIMS OF THE NANTIINAQ 49

CHAPTER 9 PORT CHATHAM TIMELINE 54

CHAPTER 10 TOM LARSON'S TALE 58

CHAPTER 11 PARANORMAL PORT CHATHAM 62

CHAPTER 12 CHANCE ENCOUNTER OR FATE? 67

CHAPTER 13 THE 2018 PORT CHATHAM EXPEDITION 71

CHAPTER 14 THE 2019 PORT CHATHAM EXPEDITION 99

CHAPTER 15 LIVING HISTORY 120

CHAPTER 16 THE LEGEND LIVES 129

CHAPTER 17 MORE SIGHTINGS ON THE KENAI PENINSULA 132

CHAPTER 18 THEORIES AND CONCLUSIONS 135

SPECIAL ACKNOWLEDGMENTS 140

REFERENCES 141

CHAPTER 1
THINGS THAT GO BUMP IN THE WOODS

I was miserable. What had started out as a short afternoon hike, had turned into me being drenched from the waist down and freezing. It was October, and I was outside, wet and in Alaska. Not an ideal combination. The temperature was a tepid 45 degrees and it was cloudy. I was getting cold. I knew from experience; I was not anywhere close to being hypothermic. I had been in far worse situations before but that did not stop me from acknowledging how physically uncomfortable I was at the present time.

We were walking on a small trail around Bottenintnin Lake near Sterling, Alaska. I had dragged my wife out to this location on a day hike and after walking less than a mile, I had ended up stepping into soft, wet, marshy turf that comprised most of the local terrain, falling to my hands and knees. As usual, my wife was more prepared than I was and had worn tall, waterproof boots. I had worn my usual attire of jeans and hiking shoes. After getting soaked the last time I was in the area, I had foregone actual preparedness and had just told myself I would be "more careful" this time. I was "more careful" for about twenty minutes and then, had somehow ended up in knee deep water.

I was cold, wet and disappointed. What we had planned on being a several hour hike, had turned into about a forty-five-minute trek. Plans to reach the far side of the lake had to be quickly abandoned after I had inadvertently soaked myself from feet to waist. We walked closer to the lake's shore where the ground was more stable and less marshy. I knew from my previous visit to the area, there was a small trail that led around the lake to the main parking area where my truck waited, along with dry socks and warmth.

I would not label myself an "avid outdoorsman" but I had certainly been on my share of fishing, camping, hunting and hiking trips. Plus, a stint in the Army had made me very familiar with walking in wet clothing and footwear. The wet socks I wore began to slowly slide down my calf and bunch up into a cold wet mess at the top of my shoes. My feet, lubricated by the water sloshing around in my shoes, began to slide around inside my shoes and I could tell that if I did not get back to the truck soon, there would be blisters. My wet blue jeans were not faring much better, pinching and chaffing as they became heavier and harder to walk in.

As we reached the shore of the lake, the ground became firmer and the trees became thicker and more abundant. We started walking along the edge of the lake toward the parking area. There was a makeshift trail that I imagine fishermen had carved out looking for different areas and angles to cast their lines. I was back in familiar territory now and was struck with the kind of tunnel vision that only a person in cold, wet clothing heading toward warmth and safety can be afflicted with.

For me, the trek was over, I was almost back to the truck. I was thinking about how I was going to put the tailgate down, sit on it to remove my socks and shoes, and dry my feet. I was walking along the trail stepping over the occasional root, pushing aside the many branches that hung in the way. Thinking about the nice warm truck and my dry socks inside it. Yes, my hike was over. Then, something happened.

Actually, several things happened almost simultaneously.

"We are almost to the truck." I said over my shoulder to my wife. She was walking a few feet behind me. I knew the way and she was following the leader.

THUMP! THUMP! THUMP!

As I turned my head and spoke about being near the truck, I heard three distinct, deep thumps. It sounded like something heavy was striking the ground. Being afflicted with the aforementioned tunnel vision, I thought what I was hearing was my wife striking her walking stick on the ground, probing for watery holes in the moss.

"SHHHH!" my wife shushed me and turned to look behind us. "Did you hear that?" She asked.

"Yeah," I replied. "Wasn't that you hitting your walking stick on the ground?"

"No," she said. "Whatever that was, came from behind us." She continued looking back in the direction we had come. Her unease was obvious.

I immediately forgot about my wet shoes and pants. I wanted to know what made that sound. I stepped around my wife and began walking toward where I thought the sound had come from. I scanned the woods and strained my ears, listening for anything that might give me a clue where the origin of the noise was.

I placed my hand on the gun at my hip and walked even further toward where I believed the sound had come from. Nothing. Not a single clue would be found that day to give me any idea what had made that strange, hollow thumping sound. I even tried to recreate the sound by jumping up and down on the ground. I'm a big guy, well over 200 pounds and not to mention I was carrying several pounds of extra gear, plus my gun. I was also waterlogged. Even so, I could not reproduce the sound my wife and I had heard.

In my mind I went through the usual list of Alaskan suspects that may have been responsible for making such a sound, the usual culprit in many such cases are moose. I've lived in Alaska for about seventeen years. I've had more than my fair share of encounters with moose. I've almost hit them in my car, I've shot wounded ones on the side of the road, after being hit by other people's cars, I've had them in my yard eating my grass and trees, I've even seen them looking in the windows of my house. On one occasion, I had one chase my dog and I onto the porch of my house.

The problem I found in assigning this mystery sound to a moose was twofold; one, while moose can be stealthy, they generally are not. Especially when they move quickly. A fast-moving moose can sound like a freight train going through a forested area. Branches snap, leaves trampled and a literal cacophony of sounds follow the moose on its flight. Two, I did not see a moose. I walked back and saw no moose sign or any tracks in the area. Further, if a moose had caused the noise it, did not trail off into the distance and sounded like it had remained in the area. I saw no evidence that one had been in the area recently.

The second usual suspect in such matters, is usually a bear. Alaska has a few different species of bear that call it home. I am more familiar with the black bear. Like the moose, I have had several run ins with black bear. From observing them from afar, finding tracks and signs to chasing them away from garbage cans with a shotgun. I was no expert, but I knew enough about bears to know that I didn't want to mess with them and I did not want them to mess with me. My dismissal of bears as the culprit of our mystery sound was pretty similar to my reasons for ruling out moose. I had seen no bear sign in the area, and bears like to mark their territory...a lot.

There is a reason why the anecdote about what bears do in the woods is so saturated in our culture. They do their bear business in the woods often and with such frequency a person might think they were receiving commission for each job done. They especially like to mark their territory on trails. Like the one we were walking on. Bears also have a certain scent to them. You can smell them when they are close by and the wind is right. Neither my wife nor I had any reason to believe there were bears in the area. Most sensible bears were probably settling down for a long winter's nap in their dens around this time of year.

After eliminating the usual suspects, I tried assigning the strange sound to less obvious sources, I even considered that an eagle or other large bird could have caused the sound by flapping its wings while perched in a nearby tree. Again, that explanation was quickly discounted, I had felt the thuds vibrate the ground. Whatever had caused them, had been on the ground or at least touching the ground when the sound was made.

The more I thought about it, the more I began to believe that the originator of the strange noises we heard that day, may have been the animal I was out there trying to see in the first place. Sasquatch.

CHAPTER 2
THE GREAT SASQUATCH HUNTER

Growing up in a small rural town in Kentucky can get pretty boring. Especially in the winter. Fortunately, for me, the tiny town I grew up in had a library right across the street from my house. I read a lot. Like many kids, I especially liked to read about monsters.

The library had several of the Crestwood monster series books. I highly recommend them and suggest looking them up. While most of those books were about monsters that were in movies like *Godzilla, Dracula* and *Frankenstein*. Nestled in amongst those Crestwood monster books was one with an illustrated girl on the cover. Throughout the years, I would become infatuated with this girl. So much so, that her real-life counterpart would often become the desktop background for many of my computers, phones and tablets that I would own in the future. That girl was Patty. The star of the famous Patterson-Gimlin footage, filmed in Bluff Creek, California.

That book opened up a new world to me, a world that made the possibility of monsters real. Maybe, somewhere out there, there was a Bigfoot. If there was a Bigfoot, who knows what else could be out there? I spent much of my youth reading, researching and even occasionally hunting for Bigfoot, ghosts and any other mysterious creature that might be out there. I can confidently say that if there were any monsters or ghosts in the tiny town I grew up in, I would have found them.

Thanks to the magic of the internet, I recently came into possession of a copy of that book. I was amazed at some of the details I had in my memory and amazed at things in the book I did not remember. The book now has a permanent home on my office bookshelf in the company of many other books of similar topic, written by explorer's, scientists and those who seek the answer to mysteries.

Over the years, my interest in the subject would wax and wane, but was always there. Eventually, I got to a point in my life where I was able to do a bit of traveling. While most people my age were traveling to popular tourist destinations and getting their picture taken at the Grand Canyon or the Statue of Liberty, I was trudging through the woods in places like Salt Fork State Park in Ohio, Fouke, Arkansas and Bluff Creek, California, with a camera and a mission. I want to see one.

During my travels, I've certainly had my share of unusual experiences but nothing I can claim as a sighting. Since I can't travel all the time, I began to look into more local options for my Bigfoot fix. Through a series of events involving family and job searches, I wound up living on the Kenai Peninsula in Alaska.

At first glance, the Kenai Peninsula certainly does not seem "squatchy". In fact, a web search of Alaska sightings and a search for books on Bigfoot activity in the region, might lead a person to believe the Kenai Peninsula is the least "squatchy" place in Alaska. However, after a little research and some digging around, I found Alaska's Kenai Peninsula had a secret history that not many people are aware of. Beyond the rivers and streams teeming with salmon and beyond the tourist shops full of Alaska related merchandise, there is an expanse of wilderness capable of sustaining a creature that few believe in and even fewer have seen. Somewhere among the forests and mountains, something walks. For reasons we cannot understand or comprehend, it walks away from technology and humanity, choosing to live in isolation. Only to be seen in glimpses and spoken of in whispers.

This is a chronicle of both my physical and historical search for Bigfoot on the Kenai Peninsula. Answers were found, but as always with this topic, more questions were also raised. Zip up your coat, lace up your boots, and come with me on an adventure, as we explore the history and horror of Port Chatham, Alaska.

CHAPTER 3
ALASKA'S PLAYGROUND

The Kenai Peninsula is a large peninsula that extends from the south-central portion of the state. The peninsula gets its name (pronounced Keen Eye) from the indigenous people that live in the area, the Kenaitze Tribe. Most of the settlements, both native and otherwise, were often based on or around the rivers and oceans which produce bountiful amounts of fish. In 1957, oil was discovered on the peninsula and today the Kenai Peninsula's mainstays of employment include fishing, oil and tourism.

As landmasses go, the Kenai Peninsula has a lot crammed into a small package. The peninsula is a mere 150 miles long, a relative pittance in Alaska standards. However, inside those 150 miles is a veritable smorgasbord of terrain and environs. Contained on the peninsula are mountain ranges, glaciers, ice fields, boreal forests, marshes, tundra, lakes of all sizes and even an expansive coastline with beaches. One could say there is something for everyone on the Kenai Peninsula.

Among all these terrains and environs, there are protected areas such as the Kenai Fjords National Park and the Kenai National Wildlife Refuge. The Kenai National Wildlife Refuge alone is a

1.92-million-acre area of protected land, some of which is only accessible by plane or boat. It's safe to say, there are areas of the peninsula that have never been tread on by humans.

The Kenai Fjords National Park covers an area over 600,000 acres, mostly glaciers that extend from the Harding Ice Fields. This area, along with the Kenai National Wildlife Refuge, make the Kenai Peninsula one of the most protected areas in the country in which wildlife is allowed to thrive.

Along with the wildlife refuges and National Parks, there are also large areas of land that are privately owned by native tribes and corporations. Much of this land is undeveloped and special permission is needed from the tribe to even set foot on it. These areas make up some of the most remote parts of the Kenai Peninsula.

The Kenai Peninsula has a few nicknames but the one most often used is "Alaska's Playground." This name comes from the number of activities and locations available for recreation on the peninsula. Alaskans and tourists alike flock to the peninsula from Alaska's largest city, Anchorage, to partake in fishing, hiking, hunting and other outdoor activities. Being within easy driving distance of Anchorage, puts the peninsula at the top of many tourists lists.

Population wise, the Kenai Peninsula is sparsely populated at best. Only four first class cities are located on the peninsula and the most populous only has just over seven thousand people. In fact, the entire peninsula only boasts a population of 58,000, less than most mid-sized cities in the lower 48 states. That's a lot of elbow room. Lots of room for moose, bear and other things.

In 2015, two large brown bears were killed by hunters on the Kenai Peninsula, one weighed in at 974 lbs and the other at 880 lbs. Those weights are after the removal of the hide, head and some of the meat (Bragg, 2015). The existence of animals of that size certainly creates a precedence that the Kenai Peninsula is capable of sustaining large animals.

In 2011, a 600 lb black bear was killed in the middle of the city of Homer by local police. The bear had been raiding the grease traps of a local restaurant near the town's main street. Again, this shows that the peninsula is capable of producing and sustaining large animals. If a bear that large could be sneaking around in the second largest city on the peninsula, what else could be lurking out there in the vast expanse of undeveloped wilderness?

CHAPTER 4
PORT CHATHAM, ALASKA
1931

Andrew Kamluck wiped the sweat from his brow using his untucked flannel shirt. It was hot and he had been exerting himself all day, it would be getting dark soon. He walked over to the stump he was using as a makeshift work table and picked up his thermos of water, he took a long swallow of water and then poured a bit on his head.

During his brief respite, Andrew looked around and surveyed the work area. He had gotten here just after breakfast and had been working almost nonstop. Andrew checked his watch, it was almost seven in the evening, he had to get home to his wife and son. He was supposed to have help. He and two other men from town had gone in together to start this logging operation and make some money. They had all agreed it was a good way to get out of the fish cannery and go into business for themselves. Plus, they got to work outside and shoot the occasional moose or Dall sheep that wandered into their work area, adding to the food on their tables. All in all, it seemed like a win-win situation.

However, three months in, Andrew found himself out in the woods alone. His partners had begun to spend less and less time at the worksite, and most days, Andrew found himself here alone. Initially, his partners had given excuses about their absence, family members had been sick, neighbors needed help with this or that, then his partners had just stopped giving excuses. They didn't have to, Andrew knew why they were not here, they were scared.

For a few weeks, Andrew had been able to hire a few men from the town to help him out. It did not take long for the number of willing laborers to dwindle down to zero. Between word of mouth and personal experiences...no one was willing to come this deep into the woods to cut wood.

It had started innocently enough; the men would show up to work and place their supplies for the day down in a shady area. Lunches, snacks, thermoses and tools would be placed under a shady tree or next to a rock. When you work in the woods, there are no ice chests, break rooms or locker rooms to store your possessions. The men would go to retrieve their items and find them missing.

At first, the men had blamed each other for the missing items. It was chalked up to general hazing and practical jokes. Eventually, the men realized no one at the worksite was responsible and the blame was shifted to bears or mischievous varmints. That is, until events became too bizarre to explain.

Andrew and his partners would show up to work to find large logging chains broken, axe handles would be found broken in two as if split like a toothpick. Andrew thought that someone was trying to run them off in order to take over their logging area. His partners were less inclined to believe this and blamed the eerie events on the hairy man, a creature the natives called the Nantiinaq. Andrew did not know what to make of it. He had grown up hearing the tales of the Nantiinaq, just like his partners had, but he had been living, working and hunting around the area for several years and had never seen anything that led him to believe the Nantiinaq was real. He believed it was just a tale elders told their children to keep them from wandering off.

Andrew shook his head and took another sip of water; he couldn't continue to work the logging operation by himself. Tomorrow he was going to hitch a ride to Seldovia on his cousin's boat and try to recruit some help. Surely, he would be able to find a couple of brave souls in Seldovia that could help him finish up before winter arrived in a few weeks. Maybe, Andrew speculated, if he found two competent hard workers, he could actually take a day off and spend it with his wife and son.

Andrew screwed the lid back on his thermos and placed it in his bag. He needed to get home. He turned around and walked back to the log he had been cutting on. His axe was gone.

He furrowed his brow...it had just been here before he walked over to get a drink. Andrew looked all around the log he had been cutting on, thinking the axe might have just fallen over and was laying on the ground. How could this happen? He had only been fifteen feet away drinking his water.

Andrew was angry, he couldn't afford to keep buying axes! It had gotten so bad; the men had started taking their axes home at the end of the day. Now, he couldn't even find it to take it home. Andrew threw his pack on the ground. He wasn't going home until he found his axe.

He hunched over and began to study the ground around the log. The ground was spongy and soft, not good for tracks, he could only make out the impression he himself had made. Dismayed, he looked up to the sky. Did the axe fly away? Was it taken by an eagle?

Frustrated, Andrew spun around, looking for any clue that could lead him to his axe. Finding nothing, he called out in anger.

"Leave me alone! I'm just trying to feed my family!"

As if in response, Andrew heard a cry from the tree line behind him.

"Ooowoop! Ooowoop!"

Andrew spun around just in time to see a black shape dart between two trees. Andrew squinted. It looked like a bear. But it was on two legs!

To his left, Andrew heard a sharp explosive sound, like someone hitting a baseball bat on a tree trunk. He spun his head in that direction and saw nothing. Then, *Crack! Crack! Crack!* to his right. Andrew's head was on a swivel, looking toward the knocks, looking to where he had seen the dark blur. He saw nothing.

Behind him, Andrew heard voices, he couldn't make out what they were saying, it sounded like gibberish. No words spoken, but he recognized the tone, one of the voices sounded deep and angry, the other, was higher pitched, almost plaintive. Andrew thought it sounded close to when he and his wife argued, only it wasn't in English and it was coming from deep in the forest.

Another black blur dashed between two trees. Andrew got a better look at this one. It looked like a hairy man! A great flood of realization washed over Andrew Kamluck, it was in this moment he realized all the stories the elders had told him were true, the Nantiinaq was real and it was here! He racked his brain trying to remember a story or word of advice he had received about dealing with the Nantiinaq, but he couldn't recall ever hearing any…or if he had he had not bothered to remember it.

Andrew's knees began to shake. He spun around and began to run toward the path back to town. Andrew began to form a plan, he would get to the path, run as fast as he could back to the cannery. Once at the cannery, he would find the foreman, drop to his knees and beg and plead for his job back. If anyone was foolish enough to come up here for his equipment, they could have it, he was never coming into the woods again!

His weariness from the days' work was forgotten, his legs pumped underneath him getting him closer to the path…to safety. He was almost there, he just had to keep going.

From his left, he heard a whirling sound, like something was traveling through the air at a high velocity. He glanced to his left and saw a large rock hurtling toward him, on a path to intersect with him. He skidded to a halt and the rock sailed past him, inches from connecting with his head.

Andrew looked to the left from where the rock originated, he squinted his eyes trying to focus in the darkness between the trees. It was then that he saw it. It was huge, shoulders twice as wide as his own and at least seven feet tall. It was amazing. If it had not been moving, Andrew doubted he would even be able to see it. Between steps, when it was still, it seemed to almost meld with the background, perfectly camouflaged for an instant until its movement gave it's form away. The black sinewy hair almost matching with the bark, leaves and brush.

Andrew stared; it was coming toward him. As it got closer, he could hear it breathing; long, labored breaths. Its eyes were solid black but glimmered red when the sun poked through the thick canopy. The Nantiinaq pulled its lips back exposing huge teeth. The creature began to walk faster toward Andrew, almost at a jogging pace. Andrew instinctively began to back up.

The creature sped up even more, Andrew quickened his backward retreat. Suddenly, the creature stopped a few feet from Andrew and opened its mouth, exposing a pink tongue and black throat…the creature roared. It was louder than any machine or beast that Andrew had ever heard. The mouth on the creature kept opening as it screamed, wider and wider until the mouth was opened at an angle Andrew thought impossible.

He felt the ground vibrate and his chest rattle as the Nantiinaq stood screaming at him. Andrew continued to rush backwards until his heel hit the trunk of felled tree and he fell backwards over the log.

Andrew lost sight of the beast as he fell and struck his head on the base of a stump, he looked up, slightly dizzy, but could only see his knees bent over the log he had fallen over. The creature's scream reached a high pitch and then began to descend down, like the old air raid sirens Andrew had heard on the radio programs.

Panicked, he scrambled to get a look at the creature. Was it coming toward him? Was it picking up another rock? Unable to get to a standing position, Andrew used the log as cover and swung his legs over it so he was lying behind it. He slowly peeked his head over the log as the scream faded off into silence.

The creature was gone.

Andrew looked around as best he could, his head hurt and he had tears in his eyes and his nose was running uncontrollably. He saw nothing. Still laying on the ground behind the log, he took a moment and wiped his face and nose with his shirt, trying to form a plan of escape. First, he would get up from behind the log and continue to the path, starting out at a quick walk. Maybe running from the Nantiinaq was bad, like running from a bear?

He steeled himself, fighting against paralyzing fear, and placed his hands on the ground and began to push himself up. He heard a sound, behind him, it sounded like metal being hit against metal.

Andrew got to his feet and spun around. What he saw he could barely comprehend. Standing not thirty feet from him was another Nantiinaq. This one was not black like the other, it was gray and had a stripe of hair that stuck up on the middle of its head like a mohawk. It was also considerably bigger than the black one, it looked older, and angrier. Andrew saw that the creature was holding the log skidder over its head!

The log skidder weighed at least 400 pounds. It had taken Andrew, his two partners and another two men from town to get it off the boat when it had been delivered. How the creature was able to lift it seemingly without effort was incredible.

The creature walked toward Andrew with purpose; log skidder held over its head. It didn't scream like the black one. It just stared at Andrew as it stalked toward him, a look of utter disgust upon its face. As each foot fell upon the ground, Andrew felt the concussion of the combined weight of the Nantiinaq and the log skidder reverberate in his chest.

The creature reared back and hurled the log skidder toward Andrew. Time slowed down for Andrew as the log skidder flew through the air toward him. His last thoughts were of his wife and child, he prayed that they would be able to escape Port Chatham without ever seeing the Nantiinaq.

CHAPTER 5
A TREASURE TROVE OF NATURAL RESOURCES

On the southern tip of the Kenai Peninsula, there is a small, protected bay that few people know about, and even fewer visit. Royal Navy Captain, Nathaniel Portlock was one of the first to explore the area in 1786. Captain Portlock wrote in his logs how impressed he was with the number of natural resources in the area. The area was rich with virgin timber, coal seams and abundant fishing grounds.

In 1791, English explorer George Vancouver came through and mapped the bay, naming it for one of his ships, the HMS Chatham. The area was also frequented by Russians who came to the area in search of otter and other furs as well as sheltering in the bay during storms.

In the early 1900's, an American company brought a fleet of fishing vessels in the area to take advantage of the ample halibut, salmon and other sea life. Because of the calm waters, Port Chatham was chosen as the location to build a cannery to process and prepare the local catch for commercial distribution.
I can only imagine the amount of work that went into the construction of the cannery and worker housing. Not only was it

the early 1900's and the technology and equipment was not like it is today, they were moving into virgin land that had never been cleared or built on before. Having been to the area (more on that later) and having seen how incredibly thick and primordial the terrain is, I can only shake my head and think that back then, people were made of tougher stuff.

The fishing fleet was a great success and the cannery was in need of workers. The company brought in local Aleut Natives to work in the cannery. Records from the time are incredibly difficult to come by and researching the history of Portlock/Port Chatham can be quite the daunting task. In my research, I've been unable to discern how many workers the cannery employed but from what I can infer from the tales and stories, it was a substantial amount.

During the halcyon days of operation, a cold storage facility was built in Port Chatham. Records are devoid of intricate detail however; I have found documentation that the facility was built to handle 200,000 lbs of halibut.

The general consensus is that there were two towns in Port Chatham Bay. The town of Port Chatham and the town of Portlock (named for Captain Nathaniel Portlock). I have not been able to find any maps that show the two towns or how far apart they were. Documents from the era seem to use the names Port Chatham and Portlock interchangeably. For the purposes of this work and to keep things simple, I will simply refer to the town(s) as Port Chatham (No disrespect intended to Captain Portlock).

Along with the fishing, Port Chatham also rewarded the brave souls that explored it, with other natural resources. Coal seams were mined and a chromite mine was established in the area. Chromite is a mineral that has many commercial and industrial uses, including but not limited to the manufacturing of stainless steel and porcelain tiles. The mine in Port Chatham, often referred to as Chrome, was once a bustling industrial center. Between the years of 1917-1918, 1,000 tons of hand sorted ore was shipped out to aid in manufacturing during World War I. Records from the era describe as many as 25 natives working for the mine around that time period. After the war, the price of chrome fell and the mine did not last much longer after that.

Along with the bountiful resources under the ground, the topside of the soil teemed with resources as well. Over the years, several sawmills and logging operations of various sizes and repute operated in the area. With a landscape of trees as far as the eyes can see, it is no wonder the area was valued by logging companies and independent loggers alike.

The town, in its heyday, was a bustling community for a small village. Records from the era indicate there were fox and mink farms as well as a store, post office, school (that went to eighth grade) and a pool hall. It is hard to imagine, knowing that there was so much industry and infrastructure in the area, that by 1950, the area would be devoid of all human life, left to be reclaimed by nature. The general consensus is; the Postmaster was the last resident to depart the town in 1950. Despite mankind's best efforts to tame and control Port Chatham, the land was able to break the will of man and loose the shackles of civilization.

Ghost towns are not an uncommon thing in the United States. Just about anyone with a casual interest in history can recite a tale of a town that was established based on the proximity to a valuable resource, usually gold or silver and how that town experienced an influx of settlers and miners, looking to profit, exploit or just plain survive using the resources available. Alas, as the Earth gives, it can also take away and even the most bountiful mine can play out. Once the local mine stops producing and the town's cash flow diminishes, the town would cease to exist. Residents would move on to greener pastures, leaving buildings and other things too big or expensive to move to be reclaimed by nature.

The history of Port Chatham can certainly be compared to the before mentioned ghost towns. Resources discovered, plundered, and people moved on. However, there are additional circumstances surrounding Port Chatham that should not be ignored. Unlike most ghost towns, the monsters and spirits seemed to have been there long before the town was abandoned.

CHAPTER 6
THE NANTIINAQ

Most, if not all, Alaskan Native tribes have tales of some sort of hair covered, upright walking creature. Some tribes even have more than one. For the indigenous people around Port Chatham, the name for their creature is; Nantiinaq (pronounced Nan-tah-knock). Depending on where you look, you may find it spelled and pronounced differently. Most native cultures depend on oral storytelling as a way of cataloguing their history and it is often left to the transcriptionist's discretion how such words are spelled. For the purposes of this work, I have settled on using the word "Nantiinaq."

Much like spelling, the translation of Nantiinaq, also seems to have multiple options. I have read and heard it translated several different ways. Some say it means "giant hairy thing" some say it means "half man half beast" while still others will tell you, "It does not translate well" and say there is no direct translation to English. Personally, I like the idea that there is no direct translation. Much like the creature itself, the very name of it, is in many ways, a mystery.

Like the very land it is said to inhabit, the Nantiinaq is not easy to research. Other than a few scattered sighting reports and some native tales, not much is known about the elusive Nantiinaq. I will do my best to relay the information I have come across.

Native elder, Malania Kehl tells a story in which a group of hunters were out in their boat, near Dogfish Bay. One of the hunters was asleep near the bow of the boat and awoke, telling the others to drop him off on the beach in the bay. After debarking the little boat, the hunter told his companions not to wait for him and that he was going to go into the woods to live with the Nantiinaq.

The man was later seen near the town of Port Graham and he told those that saw him to tell his wife to stay inside and not venture out because he might take her away. The hunter said he wanted her to stay here and watch the children. He also told them, that he was going to be in the area for a long time and he did not want the people to see him because he would be changing into "thick fur."

After that, it was said the man turned into a Nantiinaq and lived near several lakes in the area before finally moving to an area near Dogfish Bay. It was said that eventually, when the man was spotted again, he could not be understood because he was whistling and that was how he talked now. He told his friends that they were lucky that they did not become a Nantiinaq because now he could no longer understand human speech.

It was said that as the population of Port Graham dwindled, the man, now a Nantiinaq, came back and was sometimes seen near the airstrip. Hunters who went out to duck hunt said they could hear the Nantiinaq whistling in the forest.

The tale continues that a group of hunters were out one day and heard the Nantiinaq whistling and one of the hunters whistled back. The hunters then saw a bear come out across a lagoon from them and the bear began charging at them. The hunters then bit and spit on the crosses they wore around their necks and flung the crosses behind them onto their backs and ran away. (*Author's note: this is possibly to invoke some sort of divine protection*) When the hunters got back home, the hunter who had whistled back, got very ill. The ill hunter was anointed, told to drink holy water and presumably recovered.

After these events, the Nantiinaq was said to move to Second Lake, a lake near the village of Port Graham, and was seen by many people, especially the hunters. People around the village began to suspect that the Nantiinaq was taking their cats and eating them, as cats from the village began to mysteriously disappear.

When asked if this was the same Nantiinaq as the hunter who transformed, Malania states that it is and he keeps coming to the village. When asked if there was a particular lesson attached to this tale or if the tale was told during a specific time of the year, Malania said that the children were not allowed to go out unless the adults went with them and were warned not to go out alone. (Kehl, 2014)

As you can surmise from this tale, the natives believe the Nantiinaq is something different than natural creatures like moose and bear. The belief of humans turning into wild men or creatures is a common theme among many Bigfoot legends. The Kushtaka and the Wendigo are examples of similar creatures that were once human and were either kidnapped and transformed or became feral with hunger.

Portlock resident Sergius Moonin recalled a tale of seeing the Nantiinaq in 1923 when he was sixteen or seventeen years old. Sergius stated that he and his girlfriend were walking out to check fish traps, when they heard a piercing, ear splitting whistling that intensified until their ears were ringing. Sergius' girlfriend insisted they leave the area. A week later, Sergius and his girlfriend were walking toward a creek when they heard someone walking on the beach, they looked and saw the Nantiinaq walking along the beach. Sergius described the Nantiinaq as big and hairy. In a departure from many sightings of similar creatures, Sergius stated the Nantiinaq was carrying a club. Sergius' girlfriend wanted to scream but he told her to be quiet. The two returned to their parents and told them of what they had seen, but the parents did not believe them. (Evans, 1980)

Other local, native tales give the Nantiinaq more supernatural powers. In another tale, a hunter shoots a Nantiinaq and chases it into a thick copse of trees, only to find the Nantiinaq has transformed into a mouse and scurries away.

To further add to the hairy, bipedal legends of Port Chatham, I came across a book published in 1979 called *Old Beliefs* written by Feona Sawden and Tupou L. Pulu. The book is a collection of stories from the natives that live in and around the Port Graham area. Each story is in the book twice, once written in English and then again in Sugt'stun, the language of the natives. One of the tales in the book is titled *Caveman of Portlock*. As it is very short, I will include it here.

There is a caveman in Portlock.
The caveman is tall.
The caveman is hairy.
The caveman is a real person.
He didn't want to live with people.
He went to live in the forest.
Soon his clothes were worn out.
So his body became hairy.
Soon his shoes were worn out.
So his feet became big.
He did not see anyone.
He did not talk with anyone.
Soon he forgot how to talk.
He talked by whistling.
He can see you before you see him.
He will not harm you.
He is like a big bear.
If you bother him he will bother you.
This is the story of the caveman of Portlock.

This work, which was put together as a way of preserving the Sugt'stun language, certainly gives us a pretty good description of the caveman and his behavior, which closely parallels the story of the Nantiinaq. So, are the two the same? (Pulu, 1979)

No definitive physical description of the Nantiinaq exists. Most descriptions just describe it as a big hairy man. Sometimes the hair color is described as being black, other times a cinnamon reddish color. White/gray ones are also reported.

Whistling and kidnapping humans is another trait that is shared in many Native American Bigfoot legends. The similarities in the legends spread across the North American continent has always fascinated me. While it is not impossible that stories traveled across the continent by word of mouth, I've always believed the similarities in legends that transcend tribes, geography and language tend to show something more than just stories are trekking across the country.

The Dena'ina people of Alaska, who also occupied areas of the Kenai Peninsula had a similar entity in their beliefs called the Nant'ina, which translates to "the ones who steal us." Not only are the names similar, but the fear of being kidnapped by the Nant'ina is also shared. (Kalifornsky, 1991)

In the lower 48, Bigfoot inspired droves of researchers and enthusiast to take to the woods in search of the creature. In stark contrast to its lower 48 cousins, the Nantiinaq inspired quite a different reaction. While the Bigfoot of the Pacific Northwest is considered to be elusive, the Nantiinaq was said to be both elusive and deadly.

Since 1950, when the Postmaster left Port Chatham, it has been said that the town was abandoned because of the Nantiinaq and that the Nantiinaq drove the people away. Any internet search for Port Chatham will take you to dozens upon dozens of articles and videos citing local lore of the townspeople fleeing because of the murderous Nantiinaq.

One important fact to take away from the stories of the Nantiinaq, is that most of these stories predate the "Bigfoot craze" in the lower 48. So long before Jerry Crew found massive prints at a worksite and way before the Patterson-Gimlin film was captured in Bluff Creek, California, something large, hairy and on two legs was causing quite the ruckus in a small fishing town in South Central Alaska.

CHAPTER 7
THE PROSPECTOR
PORT CHATHAM, 1931

Hamish Wilson took a drag off his hand rolled smoke and tossed it to the ground. He checked the tightness on his pack mule, Bessie's harness. Satisfied, he had not forgotten anything and that Bessie was ready for the day, he took her lead and began walking into the woods.

Hamish had come to Port Chatham looking to stake a claim. He was told the area was rich in minerals and figured it was as good as any place to look for gold. Plus, other than the chromite mine nearby, no one else was working in the area. He had spent the last few days talking to locals and studying maps, trying to find the best place to look for gold. After hearing of a stream a few miles away from town, Hamish decided it was a good as place as any to start. A few of the old timers he had spoken to had told him he should stay away from the area he wanted to prospect in. They told him of some kind of "hairy man" that lived up there. The old prospector did not hold much stock in such tales, he had been exploring and looking for gold all over California and Canada and had never seen anything more dangerous than a wolverine.

Hamish trudged at a slow pace through soft spongey terrain for a long way before finally finding firmer ground and a well-traveled game trail. Leading Bessie down the trail, Hamish reflected on the directions he had received. He needed to follow this trail for a few miles and he would then be able to hear the stream and find it easily. Hamish was thankful for the long Alaskan days and figured he could work well into the early morning hours before it got too dark to see.

After a few hours of walking, the old prospector found himself where he wanted to be. A little meadow opened up off the trail and he heard and saw the stream running. Hamish led Bessie over to the stream and let her drink her fill. He then set her up with a feed bag and took a break himself and ate a small lunch that he had brought with him.

After lunch, the old prospector led Bessie to a shady spot on the edge of the meadow, at the base of a steep hill, and tied her off to a small tree. He was envious that Bessie was going to get to relax and snooze while he was doing all the work. He took the pack off of Bessie and got the tools he needed out.

It was warm, but overcast and Hamish thought that it might end up raining on him. Nevertheless, he removed his boots, rolled up his pant legs and waded out into the icy cold stream to begin panning.

A short time later, Hamish felt something small land on his shoulder and assumed the rain was about to begin. He looked up at the sky and was surprised to see the clouds had actually cleared up and it no longer looked like rain. He felt another small tap on his shoulder.

Hamish spun around and looked; he didn't see anything. Whatever had landed on his shoulder had fell into the stream with a small plop. He shrugged and went back to work in the stream, the squirrels must have plenty of nuts stored up if they are dropping them out of the trees, Hamish thought.

After working his way up the stream, Hamish decided he would go back to his pack and roll a smoke, he wasn't having much luck, but he was patient and there were miles and miles of land ripe for the picking. The old prospector waded back onto the shore of the stream and marveled at the blue hue his feet had taken on from standing in the glacial fed water.

Hamish wriggled his toes and began waddling over to his supplies to wipe off his feet. He decided he would put his socks and boots back on and let his feet warm up for a while. He bent over his pack and began to rummage in it for his thickest pair of socks, suddenly, he heard Bessie give out a loud whinny and heard a thrashing in the brush near where the mule was tied up.

Jerking his head up, he saw that Bessie was gone! Hamish blinked and stared. He knew there were bear in the area, a bear must have spooked Bessie and she took off running. Hamish rooted around in his pile of supplies and pulled out his rifle. How much time was he going to have to spend chasing down Bessie? She must have been spooked out of her mind to be able to break loose from her tether.

Still barefoot, the old prospector rushed/waddled over to where his mule had been tied, inspecting the ground for clues as to which way she must have ran. He could see where Bessie had been standing most of the day as the grasses and foliage was tamped down, but he could not see any depressions or sign that showed which direction she may have gone. He looked up and saw that the bridal reins were still tied to the tree. Walking over and inspecting them, Hamish saw they had been severed.

Hamish did not think it was possible that his old mule would be able to snap the leather reins. Maybe the bear had got lucky and swiped them with his claws or bit them? Whatever had happened, Hamish decided he wasn't going to be able to solve it barefoot. He rushed over as fast as he could on bare feet to his gear, flopped down on his backside, and began to pull on his socks and boots.

Sitting on the ground pulling up his boots, Hamish again heard whinnying and thrashing in the brush. Looking up to where the sound was coming from, Hamish saw something that shook him to his very core.

Up the steep hill, about 20 yards from where Bessie had been tethered, out of the thick alders and foliage, he saw Bessie's head poking up out of the trees. The old mule was braying, screaming and thrashing about. All Hamish could see was the old mule's face; the rest of her, as well as her mystery assailant, hidden by the thick alders and brush. The pack mule's face thrashed back and forth, the whites of her eyes flashing as she screamed.

Hamish watched in horror, as Bessie began to move up the hill at an unnatural speed. Whatever was carrying or dragging her up the hill was traversing the steep hill like it was in an elevator. Bessie's head, sticking out of the thick foliage, flew up the hill, still screaming and braying.

Hamish lost sight of her as she flew into a particularly tall copse of foliage. As soon as the braying mule was out of Hamish's sight, all went quiet. Griping his rifle tight, Hamish strained his eyes and ears in the direction of the hill, looking for any sign of the mule.

CRACK!

Hamish heard a thick, wet crack, from the copse of trees, and then nothing. The old prospector had decided that was enough. He began to frantically finish putting on his socks and boots, grabbing his rifle and his daypack, Hamish left the rest of his gear and supplies and began to hurriedly head back to the game trail.

Reaching the trail, the old prospector began heading back in the direction he had come, as fast as his frozen feet would carry him. Terrified beyond the capacity for rational thought, Hamish had no plan or strategy other than to get away from this place as fast as he could. Fortunately, the trek back to town was mostly downhill and the old prospector felt there was still plenty of daylight left to make it back.

As he rushed down the game trail, he became hyper aware of every sound, every bird call, every twig snap, filled him with a sense of dread and fear. Whatever beast or devil had been able carry off a full-grown mule, would surely be able to do the same to a man.

As he scurried down the trail, he rounded a bend and saw some distance away, a man standing on the trail. A wave of relief rushed over Hamish. At least, he thought, he wouldn't be alone.

"Hey! Over here!" Hamish shouted, waving his arms over his head. "I need help, over here! Something got my mule!"

The man was too far away for Hamish to make out any details. But he was sure the man had heard him because as Hamish shouted, the figure tilted its head, in the same manner a dog would, when it hears a strange noise. Hamish began to walk quickly toward the man, hoping to find strength in numbers. He would gladly pay the man to accompany him back to town.

The silhouetted figure raised its head and let out a bellowing yell. Hamish stopped abruptly in his tracks, his newfound relief dropped to the pit of his stomach and stagnated. The figure began to move quickly toward the old prospector. Hamish fumbled with his rifle and readied it for a shot.

Shaking, Hamish leveled his rifle and tried to draw a bead on the quickly advancing figure. As the figure began to encompass his sights, it disappeared off the trail into the foliage. It moved so unnaturally, like it had been pulled sideways by a rope, into the trees. Hamish lost sight of the figure as it disappeared off the trail.

Hamish was frantic, he did not know what to do, should he turn back? Should he continue forward? Indecisive, Hamish gripped his rifle tight and bowed his head, standing in the middle of the narrow game trail, the old prospector recited every prayer he could remember and swore that if he made it out of here, he would never lust after women or partake of alcoholic drink ever again.

The old prospector stood in the middle of the trail for a good while. Praying, listening and griping his rifle tight. Time lost all meaning, unsure if he had been there 5 minutes, or 5 hours, Hamish decided he had no other choice but to continue on. He did not know any other way to get back to town other than the way he had come. Silence permeated the trail. Neither bird nor bug was making a sound. Only Hamish's own labored breathing touched his ears.

Steeling himself, Hamish made a decision, he gripped his rifle tight, and began to tepidly walk forward.

Hamish Wilson was never seen nor heard from again. A halfhearted search was conducted by a few men from the village but nothing was found. Most knew what his fate had been and figured it was best if what was left of him, was not found.

CHAPTER 8
THE VICTIMS OF THE NANTIINAQ

While the previous chapter's tales of Andrew Kamluck and Hamish Wilson are dramatized, they are, in fact, based on real life events. No one knows exactly how many alleged victims of the Nantiinaq there are, but local tales puts the number around at least three to five on the low side. Personally, I believe the number would have to be higher, probably in the double digits.

For the area to receive the reputation it has garnered, I surmise that it would take more than just a couple odd deaths and disappearances to drive people away from the resource rich Port Chatham.

Andrew Kamluck was found dead near his logging operation. It was said that he had been struck with a large piece of logging equipment too heavy for a person to lift. Andrew's family blamed his death on the Nantiinaq. *(Andrew is actually related to Malania Kehl from the previous chapter.)*

As lacking in details as the story of Andrew Kamluck is, it gives us one thing more than most tales of the Nantiinaq, a name. Having worked in law enforcement for some time, I got excited at the possibility of having an actual name of a victim of the Nantiinaq. Knowing Andrew's name, I could hopefully find records of his death. I did not hold a lot of hope for finding any case files or investigative notes, but I thought one thing I would be able to find would be his death certificate, which would list a cause of death. If nothing else, it would collaborate or disprove the tale surrounding his death.

I searched through hundreds of online documents without success. I finally conceded that the document(s) I sought may not be online so I enlisted help at the Alaska State Archives in Juneau. I worked several days with a nice lady from the archives. After explaining to her what I was looking for and why I was looking for it, she seemed just as excited as I was to help me in my search.

Ultimately, we ended our search without finding Andrew Kamluck's death certificate. However, we did not walk away completely empty handed. We found a death certificate for Willie Anahonak, who drowned in Port Graham when he was 14 years of age. The significance of Willie's death certificate is that it lists his place of birth as Portlock and his father is listed as Andrew Kamluck.

Willie was born in Portlock to Andrew Kamluck in 1927. This was not necessarily the information I was looking for, but it's significance should not be overlooked. This document proves that Andrew Kamluck did exist and was living in Portlock/Port Chatham in the late 1920's. That doesn't collaborate the circumstances or manner of his death, but it does put him in the right place at the right time. Not the evidence I was looking for but evidence, nonetheless.

I can only speculate as to why there is no death certificate for Andrew Kamluck in the state archives. I could easily blame the lack of a death certificate for a suspected victim of the Nantiinaq on some grand conspiracy perpetrated by the government to hide the truth. The reality of the situation is most likely much more mundane. Record keeping in small rural communities in Alaska has never been that reliable and events that occurred before statehood and mandated record keeping can be difficult, if not impossible to find. Those factors, plus the harsh, rugged environment. Fires, floods and snow burdened roofs collapsing, there are any number of reasons as to why there is no death certificate for us to find today. Chances are that there is one out there somewhere, tucked in between the pages of a family bible or in the archives of a village church or city hall.

Other alleged victims of the Nantiinaq are much more anonymous. The tale of Hamish, is based on a real life, unnamed prospector who did venture into the wilds surrounding Port Chatham, never to return. Port Graham elder, Simeon Kvasnikoff explained to the Homer Tribune in a 2009 article, "This one guy over there had a little place where he was digging for gold," Kvasnikoff said. "He went up there one time and never came back. No one found any sign of him." Kvasnikoff said he remembered the Nantiinaq was blamed for the disappearance of the miner. This was alleged to have happened around the same time that Andrew Kamluck died.

Even if you take the Nantiinaq out of the picture, there are any number of things in Alaska that can kill a man, causing them to disappear into the woods, never to be seen again. With no more information on the prospector who disappeared, all we can do is speculate. The local population attributed his disappearance to the Nantiinaq, maybe they knew something we don't? Given the proximity in time to Andrew's demise, it will certainly make you wonder, what was going on in Port Chatham in 1931? (Klouda, 2009)

Along with Andrew Kamluck and the nameless prospector, other victims are attributed to the Nantiinaq. Locals say that sheep hunters who went up in the hills to hunt the sheep never returned. No firm dates or names are ever given when the hunters are discussed. It's unknown if it was a group of hunters or multiple instances of lone hunters who met their end in Port Chatham. A number of articles that were published on Port Chatham mention that bodies would wash into a nearby lagoon and were, "mutilated in a way that a bear would not do." This is often attributed to being the bodies of hunters but no real details are given. With sparse details available on the victims of the Nantiinaq, our best available data is historical records and eyewitness accounts.

CHAPTER 9
PORT CHATHAM TIMELINE

In the course of my research, I began placing the events that occurred in Port Chatham in chronological order. I believe this is the first time the sightings and events from the area have been placed in a chronological timeline. The following timeline is made up of the events and sightings that I was able to document. It is in no way meant to be taken as a complete listing of the events and sightings. I am confident there are many sightings out there that are still untold, either from fear of ridicule and disbelief, or just from a lack of knowledge of where to report them. I fear many other accounts are lost to time, taken to the grave by the witnesses.

1786 - Captain Nathaniel Portlock sails through the area, writing about the abundant natural resources in his ships log.

1791 - Commander George Vancouver explores the area, mapping the bay and naming it after one of his ships, the HMS Chatham.

1905 - Native workers at the fish processing plant walk off the job because of "something in the woods." Seafood company brings in armed security to protect the area to bring the workers back.
~Alaska Sportsman's Magazine (1935)

1923 - Sergius Moonin and his girlfriend hear loud whistling and then a week later spot a large hairy, bipedal creature walking on a beach. (Evans, 1980)

1931 – Mysterious death of Andrew Kamluck, who is killed when struck in the head by an extremely heavy piece of logging equipment. (Klouda, 2009)

1931 – Prospector goes missing while searching for gold in Port Chatham. (Klouda, 2009)

1940's - Tom Larson spots Nantiinaq on a beach eating fish out of a fish trap. ~sasquatchtracker.com

1948 - Large human-like tracks are found. Hunters found mutilated. ~sasquatchtracker.com

1949 - 18-inch tracks found following moose tracks. Signs of a struggle and moose tracks end. 18-inch tracks continue up the mountain. ~sasquatchtracker.com

1950 - Town is abandoned, the last resident, the Postmaster, leaves in 1950.

1968 - Hunter chased out of a gully. ~sasquatchtracker.com

1973 - Hunters take refuge from a storm and hear something that sounds bipedal walking around their tent for two nights in Dogfish Bay. ~Alaska Adventure Journal Online

1973 - Article published in Anchorage newspaper. A retired school teacher was interviewed who had taught in Port Chatham during WWII. She told of cannery workers who went into the mountains to hunt sheep and bear and never returned. ~Alaska Magazine (April, 2016)

1980's - Hunters "screamed" at. ~sasquatchtracker.com

2014 - Trees shaken by seemingly invisible force after Bigfoot researcher plays recording of baby crying. Researcher told of white Bigfoot seen in the area by locals in Nanwalek. ~Report received by Author August 2019.

2018 - Extreme Expeditions Northwest, LLC travels to the area to film a documentary and search for the Nantiinaq.

2019 - Extreme Expeditions Northwest, LLC returns to the area to film a television show and again search for the Nantiinaq.

CHAPTER 10
TOM LARSON'S TALE
PORT CHATHAM, 1940'S

It was early, but Tom didn't mind. He had plenty of chores to do today before he planned to head into work. Tom stepped out the front door of his little cabin and pulled his hat down, it was drizzling rain but warm out. He stooped down and pulled a big basket out from under the steps. First on his chore list, was to head out to his fish trap and collect the salmon that had been caught and bring them home to clean.

Tom walked briskly down the path behind his cabin to the stream. The stream was a few hundred meters behind his cabin and Tom always appreciated the ease and accessibility of having fresh fish, just out his backdoor.

Tom rounded the bend in the trail and came out of the wood line, looking toward the spot in the little stream where his fish trap lay. Tom came to an abrupt stop. Standing over his fish trap, was a bear. Several times, Tom had come to tend to his trap to find it had been raided by a bear but never had he actually caught the bear in the act. Tom cursed himself for becoming complacent and leaving his rifle at home. He was just about to turn back to his cabin and get his gun when he noticed something peculiar.

The "bear" was holding the fish trap up with one paw and reaching in with the other to pull the fish out. Tom noticed the bear did not have claws or a snout, but instead, was grasping the fish much like a person would, by the tail with fingers. Tom watched as the creature lifted the fish up to its mouth and began to chew on it, eating it bones and all.

Tom realized he must be looking at the hairy man the natives were telling him about. Tom had not believed the tales, but here it was. Suddenly, Tom had an idea, if he could get back to his cabin and get his rifle, he could shoot the hairy man and prove it was real. Maybe even sell the body for a lot of money.

Tom quietly took a few steps back and sat his basket down, walking as softly as he could until he was sure he was out of earshot, then breaking into a run back to his cabin for his rifle.

Retrieving his rifle, Tom quickly rushed back to the stream. Rounding the bend, Tom was delighted to see the hairy man was still crouched over the trap, chewing almost absent mindedly on fish. Tom figured the sound of the stream must have masked the sound of his initial approach.

Tom raised his rifle to his shoulder and took a couple more steps toward the creature. At this range, there was no way he could miss! Tom had shot much smaller animals at longer ranges than this. Tom willed himself to stop shaking and used his thumb to cock the hammer on the old rifle.

The *click* of the hammer did not go unnoticed by the hairy man, and the creature wheeled around, still crouched, half eaten salmon still in its hand. Its eyes fixed on Tom, before traveling to his gun, becoming fixed on the firearm.

Tom's finger began to squeeze the trigger, like it had a hundred times before, focused on the beast at the end of the barrel. As he started to put pressure on the trigger, Tom noticed the creature's face. He noticed how it stared at his gun and saw a wave of what he could only describe as sadness, wash over the hairy man's face.

Tom released the trigger, it looked so human. It looked sad. Tom had shot all manner of creatures from squirrel to bear but had never once seen a creature with such human emotion on its face.

Tom kept the rifle trained on the hairy man and backed away, finding the trail back to his cabin, Tom walked backwards for several yards, rifle still up and at the ready, until he was satisfied the hairy man was not following him. Tom then turned and walked back to his cabin.

CHAPTER 11
PARANORMAL PORT CHATHAM

Nantiinaq is not the only mystery the residents of Port Chatham had to contend with. Along with the Nantiinaq, there were other, more supernatural denizens of Port Chatham. Much like other areas with sinister history and legend, multiple entities have been said to haunt the area of Port Chatham.

Perhaps one of the most mysterious is the Dark Lady. In an interview with the *Homer Tribune* in 2009, Malania Kehl said of the mysterious spirit; "Her dress was so long, she would drag it. She had a very white face and would disappear into the cliffs." (Klouda, 2009) Other than Malania Kehl's mention of the Dark Lady, I have found no other collaborating sources or sightings. The Dark Lady's origins and motivations are either lost to time, or hidden behind a wall of silence.

One particularly, unsettling tale comes from a hunting party from long before the white man had settled in the area. A group of hunters were out in Kachemak Bay, not far from Port Chatham, and had been returning from a hunt. The hunters were paddling along in their bidarka, a small canoe like boat, when they observed another bidarka of hunters not too far away.

The hunters were perplexed because they did not recognize the other group of hunters from any other nearby villages. The hunters began paddling their bidarka toward the group of strangers to say hello and find out where they had come from. As the hunters paddled toward the strangers, the strangers began to furiously paddle away from them as if they were attempting to elude them.

This made the hunters even more curious as they wondered why the group of strangers would be frightened of them. The hunters were young and strong and were able to paddle their bidarka faster, eventually catching up to the strangers.

As the group of hunters pulled alongside the stranger's bidarka, the strangers faced away from them and refused to look at them. After some time, the hunters were able to convince the strangers that they meant them no harm and just wanted to greet them, the strangers finally turned to face the young hunters.

The young hunters were shocked to see the strangers had only one eye in the center of their foreheads! The strangers explained that they lived nearby in a hidden village and did not typically associate with the local natives as they were treated badly because of their appearance.

The young hunters spoke with the strangers for some time and traded some meat with them before the parties went on their separate ways. None of the young hunters ever saw any of the one-eyed people again.

Perhaps one of the most chilling stories comes from the time when Port Chatham was in it's prime of economic growth. A fisherman had just returned to the dock after a long day of fishing. He was walking down the pier to retrieve a cart to load his fish into, so he could deliver it to the cannery.

On his way to the carts, he passed three young native children who were sitting on the pier facing away from him, legs dangling off the pier. The fisherman said hello to the three children as he walked past them. He found it most odd when they did not return his greeting or acknowledge his presence, they continued to stare off into the water.

As the fisherman retrieved the cart, at the end of the pier, he decided when he walked back by the children, he would reprimand them. It was considered very rude to not acknowledge and greet your elders and the fisherman had decided he was going to give those children a little lecture about manners.

As the fisherman turned around with his cart, he was shocked to see the children were gone! They had disappeared between the time he had walked past them, grabbed the cart and turned back around. There was nowhere for the children to go and no rational explanation for what had occurred. The fisherman had not recognized the children from the village and never encountered them again. This encounter was said to have disturbed the fisherman greatly.

Along with the preceding tales, there are numbers of other superstitions and stories surrounding the area. Most locals will tell you the area is "haunted" or "evil." When pressed, they will say they have heard stories from family members or friends who have been to the area and experienced things. Few firsthand accounts are available.

In the 1980's there was a series of UFO sightings or what is commonly known in UFO circles as a "flap." Many residents around Kachemak Bay reported seeing strange lights in the sky, flying around and making unusual turns, banks and movements that conventional aircraft could not perform.

There is a ranch in Utah known as Skinwalker Ranch, it gets its name because of Native American legends in the area of a creature called the Skinwalker. I often wonder at the similarities between Port Chatham and Skinwalker Ranch. Because of their similar histories of multiple types of activities; from sightings of Bigfoot-like creatures, to strange unidentified craft flying in the sky, both have certainly had their share of strange activity. In the book, *Hunt for the Skinwalker* by Colm Kelleher and George Knapp, the new owners of the ranch are warned by the previous owners, "Don't do any digging on the property." (Colm A. Kelleher, 2005)

When I learned about the mines in Port Chatham, both coal and chrome, my mind could not help but to draw a parallel between Port Chatham and Skinwalker Ranch. Did the act of digging or disturbing the earth have something to do with the strange activities in the area? Could the reputation of Port Chatham be earned because of what resides under the ground and not in the nearby woods?

CHAPTER 12
CHANCE ENCOUNTER OR FATE?

I get asked often how I got involved with the expeditions into Port Chatham. I explained my youthful interest in the field of cryptozoology in the earlier chapters but if I had an "origin" story, this would be it. I think I can explain it in one sentence really. Adam Davies wanted a free drink.

It all started in September 2017, after finding a curious impression in the terrain near Bottenintnin Lake, and then, on our hiking trip, being "escorted" out of the woods, I was burning for answers. I was listening to podcasts and reading books and basically consuming as much info on the subject as I could. I eventually learned of the International Bigfoot Conference in Kennewick, Washington. I was due some time off and traveling to Washington was not that expensive so I decided to go. It was my first Bigfoot conference.

The lineup of speakers was phenomenal and I learned so much on the first day. I pretty much walked back to my room after the first day of speakers one hundred percent convinced that the Patterson-Gimlin film was real. I was in heaven. It was nothing but Bigfoot talk and discussion all day. One of the speakers was a gentleman that I was not very familiar with. I had seen him on television and had heard his name here and there but I wasn't too familiar with his research. Adam Davies gave an excellent talk and I was enthralled with his adventures, he was a real-life Indiana Jones!

Because it was my first conference, I had decided to go all out and I had treated myself to the VIP dinner. The concept of the dinner was that you would be able to hang out with the speakers of the conference and have a dinner with them at the end of the day. Each table had one guest speaker. I had no idea whose table to sit at. When they had opened the doors to the dinner, I had been one of the first in line and I walked into a room full of empty tables. Not knowing whose table was whose, I just picked a random table in the corner and sat down.

Not long after taking my seat, I was joined by Adam Davies and his lovely wife Nadia, as well as other attendees of the conference. The table had some very interesting conversation and I was very impressed with Adam's experiences and his grounded approach to the subject. After the conference, I had sent Adam a friend request on social media and he accepted. I was looking forward to following his adventures that he documented on his social media, not knowing how that friend request would change my life.

One day, I was perusing social media and saw that Adam had published a post about being unreachable for a few days because he was traveling to Alaska. I was intrigued because I lived in Alaska, so I messaged him and asked him where he was going. Adam informed me he was going to be doing some scouting around Port Chatham, Alaska. I was very taken aback by his answer because I was very interested in the stories surrounding Port Chatham and I also happen to live very close by. I told Adam that if he happened to find himself in Homer, to give me a call and I would buy him a drink. I gave him my phone number and he said he would give me a ring if he found himself in town.

A few days later, I was sitting on my couch after work and was looking forward to going to bed, as I had to work the next day, when my phone rang. The caller ID did not provide a name but had a California area code. I almost didn't answer, thinking it was a telemarketer. I had all but forgotten about my offer to Adam. My curiosity got the best of me and I answered. It was Adam. He was at a local hotel and wanted to take me up on my offer of a drink. I said I would meet him at the bar across the street, and my wife and I loaded up and took off to the bar.

When I got to the bar, I met not only Adam, but his associate, Stephen Major, who he had been to Port Chatham with. Stephen was a very interesting guy, a fellow military veteran and very interested in the Bigfoot phenomenon. We all sat and talked for a few hours, I told them about the local legends and terrain and they regaled me with tales of their recent and past adventures. Before parting, I got my picture taken with them outside their hotel, they were exhausted from their recent scouting trip to Port Chatham, and I was worn out from being at work all day and had to go back early the next day. We had an excellent evening and I left very much looking forward to meeting up with them again someday.

A few months later, I was contacted by Stephen. He informed me that he was headed back to Port Chatham to film a documentary and that Adam was unable to make it. He asked if I would be interested in filling Adam's spot on the team. After I picked my jaw up off the floor, I said yes. I could not believe how just a few months ago, Port Chatham had been so close, yet so far…but now I was getting invited to not only go there, but to take part in a documentary!

CHAPTER 13
THE 2018 PORT CHATHAM EXPEDITION

After being invited on the expedition I went out and purchased several hundred dollars' worth of equipment. Hindsight being 20/20, I wish I had spent more on better gear. I wish I had also spent time attempting to get in better shape physically, but the timeline did not allow it. Hiking on established trails is one thing, breaking brush through a Jurassic era rainforest is a whole different level of cardio and endurance. I learned quickly why Adam was such a dedicated runner and keeps his endurance up. Adventuring is hard work.

By the time I had been invited to take part in the Port Chatham expedition, I had already been to Bluff Creek, CA, Fouke, AR, and Salt Fork Park, OH, on my own mini expeditions. These little adventures usually just consisted of me walking around areas of sightings or activity with my GoPro and my phone and were mostly just for myself. I wasn't trying to make any sort of documentary or produce any sort of product other than the experience itself and to try and solicit a sighting.

The Port Chatham expedition was like nothing I had ever been involved in before and I was both excited and nervous. I did not want to let Stephen down and I hoped that we would be able to bring something back. This was to be the first, boots on the ground, Bigfoot research done in Port Chatham. No matter if we found anything or not, we still had the title of being the first research team to go into the area. Our expedition was going to be filmed and made into the documentary, *In Search of the Port Chatham Hairy Man.* (Martin, 2019)

I think it is important to mention that, to date, I have not made a dime off of any project I have been involved in. I've gotten a couple of free trips and meals out of them but I have never been paid for any appearance I've made in any program, documentary, conference or podcast. There seems to be a belief among the Bigfoot community, and most people, that once your face is on TV or your voice is in a podcast, that money just flows into your bank account and you light your cigars with one-hundred-dollar bills. The truth is, unless this book winds up on the NY Times Bestseller list, or I stumble my way onto the next Patterson-Gimlin film, I will never make back the money I have spent on my little "hobby" and I'm okay with that.

There is a saying among military veterans that references the "best worst days of your life," when talking about an experience like basic combat training or being deployed. I look at the Port Chatham expeditions in much the same way. You're wet, cold and hot at the same time, exhausted, hungry and you just want to go home, however, when it's over, you look back at it fondly and want to do it again.

I was ready to head to Port Chatham. I ended up taking a lot of gear I didn't need, like a tent, dehydrated food and sunblock. But it's better to have it and not need it, than to need it and not have it. Some of the extra items I took just to be prepared, and some I took due to misunderstanding of what we were doing. I was under the impression; we were actually going to be making camp and sleeping in Port Chatham. Stephen had entertained that idea but eventually decided against it.

Loaded up, we headed out on the Puk-Uk, a large boat that is usually chartered for WWII tours of the Aleutian Islands. We were told that Puk-Uk was a native term that meant to "wander" or "ramble around aimlessly," we were certainly not doing that, we had two major goals; get to Port Chatham and find the Nantiinaq.

On board the Puk-Uk, accompanying us to Port Chatham, was Stephen Major, who was the leader and coordinator of the expedition. Mary-Beth, who had a background in biology and wildlife study, and Reid. Reid had a background in geology but he was also a lifelong hunter so it was decided he would get the title of tracker as well. Josiah and his brother Toad were also along with us. Josiah was a local entrepreneur who owned his own media company. Stephen had worked with him on the recon of Port Chatham with Adam, and had hired Josiah to come along on this trip to film the documentary. Josiah had brought his brother, Toad, a family nickname, to help with the filming and to carry equipment.

The Puk-Uk pulled into Port Chatham around 0200 hours. It was dark and rainy out. Most of us were already in our bunks, trying to get some sleep for the big day when we would wake up at first light and storm the beaches of Port Chatham. Stephen, had stepped up on deck to have a smoke, and the next day, he told us that he had heard something on shore that he believed were tree knocks and vocalizations. This information gave me hope that we would have some sort of activity. I was only slightly worried that it might be the aggressive, murderous type of activity that the area was known for.

Because of my law enforcement background and the fact that I live close by and had weapons readily available, I found myself labeled as team security. I did not have a problem with this as I did have weapons training and a fair knowledge of wildlife and the terrain, but in my mind, I was one hundred percent wanting to research and look for the Nantiinaq. I wanted everyone to be safe and survive the trip, but honestly, I was not thinking about security for most of the trip.

Early the first morning, we climbed into a small zodiac, a small inflatable boat with a motor attached, and headed toward the shore. People often use the word surreal to describe many situations, but for me, as we approached the shore of Port Chatham and I knew I was about to step foot in the place I had read and heard so much about over the years, I can truly say that the moment was surreal.

As we sped toward the shore, there was the line of rocky beach that made up most of the coastline which continued up until it was broken by a wall of forest. It's difficult to describe just how thick the forest was. An almost impenetrable wall of foliage. It was a very intimidating sight.

The little boat coasted up to the shore. I can't remember which one of us actually jumped out first and placed the first footsteps on the shore. It may have been me or it may have been Josiah, with his camera ready and rolling. I do remember, stepping out of the little boat, facing the wall of trees in front of us and just walking toward it, eyes scanning the wood line for anything. I took a few steps, set down my pack and continued walking toward the wood line. I reached for my phone to start snapping pictures and realized, I still had my life jacket on! I was so enthralled with what was before me, I had forgotten to take it off when I got out of the zodiac.

Most of the foliage was literally too thick to traverse through. Of all the gear I had brought, a machete was not something I had thought to bring. We did the best we could and followed game trails toward the old townsite. At one point, ahead of us we heard the familiar *THUMP! THUMP! THUMP!* as something absconded away from our approach.

We found bear scat and tracks, as well as the usual moose scat and tracks. We also found some odd impressions that were ambiguous. At one point, we came upon an old cabin or structure that had collapsed. Curiously, near the ruins of the little structure was a collection of…well, junk. There appeared to be the back to an old

TV, a radio and other assorted pieces of junk all in a pile. When we came upon it, I was more interested in the wreckage of the old cabin, as it was the first "sign" of civilization we had found since arriving.

We filmed a bit around the old destroyed cabin and set out toward some of the still standing structures. I didn't give the junk much thought and just chalked it up to litter. Several months after the expedition, I was sitting around thinking about the trip and thinking about things, when it hit me like a ton of bricks, "Where did that junk come from?"

It's important to note two things about the junk. First, it was all post 1950's era stuff. Plastics and other more modern items were contained in the pile of rubbish. Second, we were well away from the shoreline when we found it. In fact, we were quite some ways up on the cliffs overlooking the port. If I remember correctly, we were a good 30-40 feet up away from the water. However, that junk got there, I do not believe that it was placed there through any movement of the tides or water. It may have gotten to Port Chatham by washing up on the shore but how it got to the high area where we found it, is a mystery.

I think about that pile of junk quite a bit. I wished I had photographed it more and took a better look at it. I don't remember seeing any claw or teeth marks on any of it. I doubt anyone who was littering would have bothered to lug the stuff up to the point we were at either.

We continued our slow trek through the thick foliage. Reaching an impasse, we ended up having to slip down toward the shore and follow the shoreline to get to the old townsite. Traversing the slick algae covered rocks was quite an experience. A few times, I forewent traipsing over the slick rocks and just walked through the ankle-deep ocean water. I had good waterproof boots on and I was more afraid of slipping on the slick rocks and hurting myself than I was of getting a little wet.

As we got closer to the townsite, we began to see industrial machine parts lying on the beach. Most were covered in barnacles and rust. It was weird, seeing them there. Walking along this virgin terrain, turning a corner and seeing large hundred-pound pieces of metal just lying on the beach. We would not realize it until later, but the cliffs above us was the area that housed the bulk of the machinery from the old processing plant. The pieces that we were seeing, had fallen onto the shore due to erosion, as the literal ground they sat on was chipped away over the years by the surf and tide.

Trudging along the beach, stopping to film the occasional snippet for the documentary and take the occasional picture, we finally rounded the bend and ended up near the old townsite. The townsite area I'm referring to is the area that comes up during most image searches of Port Chatham. The small cabin with the red roof that sits near the tree line in a large field.

I remember seeing the little cabin and feeling a sense of relief, it appeared it would be an easy walk through the tall grass to reach the little cabin and we planned on doing some filming and photographing around it. I looked at the small cabin as a respite from the rough terrain. It was not.

The green field surrounding the little cabin is very deceptive. It appears to be a large flat field of tall grasses. However, under the grasses, rest large logs and tree trunks which I believe may have been left over from lumber operations in the area, or placed there over the years by storms. Walking across that field was probably one of the most precarious acts of balance and traction that I have ever partaken in, and that includes any obstacle course I ever did in the military.

The logs are very difficult to see because they are covered by the tall grass. You will take two or three steps forward only to ram your toes or shin into a log. Then, you have to step up on the log to walk across it only to find the next several yards ahead are just more logs laying a few feet apart. Not only are they precariously placed apart, they are all wet from the rain and condensation from the grass. I'm not exaggerating when I say the safest way to get across that field is to crawl across the logs or perhaps strap some crampons on your feet.

After our arduous walk across the field, we finally reached the cabin with the red roof. We took a few minutes to relax and look around the little cabin. All the remaining structures we found had dirt floors. I don't know if that is the way they were built, or if the floors were just rotted away. One thing I can say about the remaining structures is that they are a credit to human construction. Most of them still kept the rainwater out and had dry dirt floors. If anything, a desperate traveler could use them to get out of the rain and dry off.

It's impressive to imagine this little cabin surviving the 1964 earthquake as well as the countless storms that no doubt batter the area. I'm very thankful that I was fortunate enough to get to explore these old structures while they still stand.

We continued on our way, into the tree line behind the old cabin, and found the ground to be a bit more stable and firmer. We found a few small trails that led to more little cabins. We placed a few trail cameras out in the areas around the most used trails. Many people criticize our use of trail cameras and point to the lack of success that researchers have had with them. I think there is a good possibility, if there are creatures such as Bigfoot in the area of Port Chatham, that they have likely never seen a trail camera before and would not know what to do about it if they saw one. That and the old adage of, "If you have something available to you and you do not use it, that's on you." Just because others had not been able to get the images they wanted; doesn't mean we would not get *something*. In the grand scheme of things, it was a cheap and easy way to have more eyes on the ground and to have them looking 24/7 in an area that had likely never had them placed in before.

We came upon the site of the old processing plant. At least that's what we assume it was. There is an area, overlooking the townsite, that has several large pieces of machinery setting out. It's a rather odd experience to be trudging through the thick, wet forest and to come out of the thicket into an area with hulking iron behemoths, silently sitting and waiting.

We explored around the machinery and took video and photographs. I'm not an engineer, nor even that much of a handyman. I could only guess what the old rusty machines were used for. One of them looked like some sort of old tractor with a seat and everything, but it appeared to possibly be the engine for some sort of belt or pulley apparatus. I would love to show someone who is familiar with that type of old equipment the photos and find out what some of those old machines really were.

Near the old machinery, we came upon an odd piece of scat. It was at least an inch and a half around and as long as Toad's size 10.5 boots. We photographed the odd scat. It did not appear to be bear scat as the bear scat we were seeing was full of berry seeds and of a different consistency, this was a long, round piece of crap. We photographed the scat and left it be. None of us wanted to carry it around in our packs and the probability of getting DNA off of scat is very low. Hindsight being 20/20, I wish we had collected it. Much later, at a conference, I was told by a gentleman that it could have been tested for parasites and it would have been quite a find if there had been parasites exclusive to primates in it. Needless to say, I now take a "poo sack" into the woods with me for just such an occasion.

It was strange to think that seventy years ago, people were making their living where I stood, working these machines to feed their families who were living in the small houses nearby. Now it was all just rusting and rotting away. Abandoned.

South of the townsite, we came upon a small lagoon. We wondered amongst ourselves if this was the lagoon that was talked about in all the legends of Port Chatham? The lagoon where the bodies had washed ashore?

Near the lagoon, Mary-Beth let us know that she had seen something that appeared to be peeking out from behind a tree. She said she wasn't sure if it was a bear or something else but it had peeked around the tree, ducked behind the tree, then peeked back out at us. Mary-Beth was the only one that saw it. We stopped in the area and used our thermal cameras to survey the area. Even though it was daylight, we felt that with the thick foliage, our thermal cameras were the best bet to see any living creatures in the thick woods.

We also heard the ground shaking, thumping a few more times on our trek around the area. Stephen mentioned that it seemed like whatever it was managed to stay just ahead of us and move too quickly for us to get a glimpse of it. Whatever it was, it was able to deftly move through the thick, rough terrain much quicker than we were.

I admit, I was initially skeptical of Mary-Beth's sighting, I thought that she may have been mistaken. However, upon further analysis, I believe she did see something. Mary-Beth is not a "Bigfoot person" and for her to describe seeing something that is commonly associated with Bigfoot behavior, "tree peeking," I think, lends to the credibility of her sighting. That and the other things that I was about to experience myself.

Another curious thing we observed, part of the landscape seemed to have plenty of bear scat and sign, we also saw lots of blueberry bushes that were picked clean. The bear scat we observed seemed to have traces of the berries in it. Those bears were doing what bears do and fattening up on the berries. However, when we got close to the area of the lagoon, where Mary-Beth had her sighting, we noticed there was no bear scat anywhere, and the berry bushes were full of nice plump berries. We would reach our hands out and grab a handful of berries and pop them in our mouths, munching on them as we trekked through the area.

There are several possible explanations for why the bears had not eaten the berries or pooped in that other area, maybe they just hadn't gotten over there yet? I have a theory that bear and Sasquatch do their best to avoid each other. I'm sure the occasional overlap in territory or dispute occurs, but I think they both do what they can to avoid each other. There is an intriguing sighting detailed in J. Robert Alley's *Raincoast Sasquatch,* in which a fisherman observes a bear come out onto a beach, as it's walking across the beach, it stops suddenly, lifts its head and sniffs the air, then runs back the way it came. Then they see a Sasquatch walking the opposite way along the beach, the Sasquatch stops, sniffs the air, then turns around and walks back the way it came. It seems like neither animal wanted much to do with the other. (Alley, 2003)

Indeed, it did seem like we had walked through some invisible line of empty berry bushes and bear poop, to full berry bushes and no bear poop.

After a few hours exploring around the old townsite and processor, and having placed a few cameras around, we decided to head back to the Puk-Uk for some lunch and to change into dryer clothes. It had been drizzling rain almost the whole time we had been out.

Back on board, Stephen took a nap, I changed clothes and rested. We wanted to avoid the area we had just explored and let our trail cameras do their thing. So, I had studied the maps and found an area, not far from the townsite where a stream flowed into Port Chatham Bay from up on a nearby mountain. I thought the stream would be a good place for wildlife to congregate and suggested it as a place we should check out.

After resting up, we again boarded the zodiac and headed to the area I had pointed out on the map. It wasn't far from where the Puk-Uk was anchored and as we approached the shore, we all saw what appeared to be tracks in the rocky shore. They appeared to come down to the shoreline and back toward the wood line.

Because of the timing of the tides, we figured that whatever had made the tracks had come down to the shoreline in the middle of the night and had quite possibly been watching the Puk-Uk from the shore, before turning around and heading back into the wood line. The tide had come and went, leaving the tracks little more than indentations in the rocky shore. Whatever had left them, was probably on the bigger side. A bear or something else?

We scrambled out of the zodiac, we removed our life jackets then Reid and I loaded our weapons, loaded weapons on an inflatable boat are not a good combination. We began to scout around the area. I followed the ambiguous impressions on the shoreline, toward the trees and up a little hill. Keeping one eye on the ground and the other on the environment around me, was no easy task. A few feet into the wood line, I saw something that made my jaw drop.

Pressed into the mossy ground was an imprint that very much resembled the shape of a human foot. Understandably, I got very excited and called for everyone to come look. Everyone shuffled over and took a peek. Some of the members of our little crew were able to see what I was pointing out, others did not. I don't even think Josiah bothered to film it, or film me talking about it.

Excited with my observation, I took several pictures. Due to the nature of the terrain, I could not get it to photograph well. I tried every trick in the book I could think of to try and get pictures of this track. I have photographed hundreds of footprints before in the course of my day job and over the years, I have learned a few tricks for making them show up better in pictures and video. Unfortunately, there was not much I could do for this track. The photographs are more of a Rorschach test than anything else. Some people see the track, plain as day, others do not.

The imprint appeared to be about 14 inches long and had the appearance of a human right foot. While no other impressions were found in the area, other than the ones on the shore, I did observe that a rotten log about 4 feet directly in front of the impression, had been disturbed and a piece of dry rotten wood had been dislodged, as if something had stepped on it.

These details should be enough to make anyone familiar with suspected Bigfoot tracks curious. While there is no absolute rulebook for identifying Bigfoot tracks, those familiar with the study of them will tell you there are certain telltale features to look for. Two of those characteristics is a four-foot-long, or more stride, as well as looking for tracks that occur in a straight line. It's theorized that, while Bigfoot walks bipedally like us, they have different shaped hips which causes their footfalls to appear to be in a straight line, not staggered, like human tracks.

Granted, all I had was an impression in the mossy ground and an askew log a few feet in front of the impression, but coupled with the history and the sightings in the area, I do not think one should discount what I found on that little trail.

We followed the trail for a while, before we ended up in a densely forested area. Again, in this area, we ran into more full blueberry bushes. Mary-Beth had the forethought to bring a large plastic bag with her and began filling the bag with berries as we explored.

At this point, I was a man on fire. I had just found, in my mind, a great track and it appeared that whatever had made it was quite possibly watching our boat from the shore. Whatever it was, we had missed it by mere hours or less. I wanted to see something! I thought we were in the right place for it.

We continued through the thick forest, toward the southeast, and ended up popping out of the thick forest into a clearing full of little pools of water. We saw a few game trails in the area leading up to the pools, and thought this would be a good area to put up a trail camera. There were moose tracks and other indiscernible tracks in the area. We were shuffling along; the ground was much easier to traverse and a welcome change.

As we were walking through this area that Stephen would later nickname, the "Valley of Death." Mary-Beth and I both, for some reason, got the mutual idea that we needed to look at a nearby wood line with our thermal cameras. I remember Mary-Beth said later that she got the feeling she was being watched. I do not recall such a feeling but I cannot deny what I saw on my thermal camera.

A little way into the wood line, I saw a figure that appeared to be on two legs and had the body shape of the video game character *Donkey Kong*. Big head, no neck, and it was moving its arms up and down as if it was agitated. I was so taken aback by what I was seeing, I passed my thermal camera over to Toad and asked him what he saw. He confirmed, it "looked like a dude." I was not able to see anything with my naked eye. Whatever it was either only showed up on the thermal camera, or was so well camouflaged behind the foliage, I could not make it out.

Mary-Beth also saw the same thing I did, only she described it as a person shuffling back and forth. Swaying is a common behavior that is reported in many Bigfoot sightings.

My thermal camera has the ability to record video. After passing my camera around to Toad, and getting it back, I finally had the idea that maybe, I should hit the record button on it.

Apparently, I waited too long between sighting the subject and hitting the record button. In the few seconds it took me to hit record, whatever it was, seemed to begin to recede into the wood line. I got footage of it, but it was not near as clear as what I had initially observed.

In my perusal of Bigfoot related media, I often heard researchers talk about the "curse of Bigfoot," this does not refer to some kind of life-threatening evil that follows a researcher around, rather it is the common name for an event that happens all too often to Bigfoot researchers. The curse usually consists of a researcher, out in the field, who has some sort of encounter only for some inexplicable event to occur so it is not documented on film or audio. Batteries die, camera's run out of memory, equipment fails or any number of similar scenarios happen.

I'm not sure if my failing to hit the record button on the thermal camera falls into the "curse of Bigfoot" category, but it certainly gave me a new perspective when hearing similar excuses for not getting better pictures or video.

I think it is important to mention, that we did get some false heat readings on the thermal cameras a few times. Often, decaying vegetation can give off heat and more than once, we would see a strange heat signature in the distance, just to find that it was an old stump that was putting off heat due to the decaying vegetation on and around it. I am confident that what I saw on my thermal camera was not an artifact of vegetation and decay. It seemed to have a defined shape that moved its arms up and down and appeared to move away from us as we approached.

We searched the area around where the thermal image had been without success. It was starting to get dark and Stephen wanted to be back on the boat before nightfall. We believed that the area we had stumbled upon was possibly our best bet for finding some sort of evidence. We hoped that our camera we had placed near the watering holes would get us an image.

I was reluctant to return back to the Puk-Uk, but I very much looked forward to some warm food and a warm bed. When we got back to the ship, Stephen and I reviewed my thermal recording. Stephen was so excited! I was too, at that point, and I couldn't wait to get back to the place Stephen was calling, the "Valley of Death." Stephen liked to make up names for areas and it helped us discern one area from another since there were no names on the map to differentiate between areas, it was all wild forest as far as the maps were concerned.

Little did we know as we crawled into our bunks that night that the "curse of Bigfoot" was not quite finished with us in Port Chatham.

The next morning, we fell into our new routine of getting breakfast and coffee, then gearing up for our adventures ashore. First order of business was to head back to the townsite and pick up the cameras we had left there the day before. Then head to the "Valley of Death" and grab our camera we had left there. Stephen was conflicted with the choice of staying another night, or leaving that evening with the tide. Since Stephen was the expedition leader and coordinator, it was his money that was on the line. The Puk-Uk was not a cheap boat to rent and another night at Port Chatham meant another two or so grand from Stephen's coffers.

We sped over to the townsite in the zodiac and snatched up the cameras. I don't recall specifically, but we may have even split up to get the cameras faster so we could get back over to the "Valley of Death" and see what our camera had in store for us.

We pulled into the same little beach area where we had inserted the day before. I did not see any fresh tracks or indentations in the gravel. Whatever had come down to the shore before, had not paid a repeat visit.

We began to head toward our trail camera and were very near the area I observed the track the day before.

As my interest began to reach a fever pitch, some of the other team member's attention spans began to plummet. Reid, Mary-Beth and Josiah were all around the same age and had many mutual interests, they began to discuss those mutual interests at a great volume in the middle of the woods in Port Chatham, Alaska.

Now, we were never trying to be very quiet. It was nearly impossible, in the primordial terrain, to walk silently. However, with the cacophony of noise coming from the millennials, it was nigh impossible to hear anything that might be in the woods around us.

Becoming aggravated by the chatter coming from the young team members, I struck out by myself and slowly began to make my way toward the game camera. I was desperate to see something and wanted to spend as much time investigating the area as I could.

I made it to the camera we had placed in the "Valley of Death." I was curious to see how many photos would be on it. I did not have the means to check the photos in the field but most trail cameras have some sort of display that will tell you how many photos are on the memory card and how many photos it can hold until full.

I reached the tree with the camera secured around it. We had selected an excellent tree that looked out into the clearing with the little freshwater pools. I figured we would, at the very least, have some footage of moose coming in and drinking out of the little pools.

I popped open the compartment on the camera and looked at the display, I was not super familiar with this camera, it was Stephen's, not mine. I could tell, though, that it was not in the correct mode to capture photos or video. The selector switch on the camera was set to the "setup" mode, which I believe was used to set the date and time, not capture pictures.

My heart sank. I felt that this camera was going to be our best bet. Based on yesterday's thermal footage and the tracks found in the area, I had high hopes that this camera would be the one most likely to capture a good image. When Stephen had placed the camera, he had placed it in the wrong mode and it had captured nothing. I was so disappointed. The "curse of Bigfoot" had struck again.

I was explaining to Josiah the situation that I had discovered with the camera when Stephen's voice came over the radio, "I swear I just saw something dart between two trees over here!"

I began to make my way over to the last place I had seen Stephen, unaware that I was actually walking toward the thing that he had seen! Because of the rough terrain, I was not able to move quickly and if there had been anything on an intercepting course with me, I'm sure it saw and heard me coming from quite a distance.

I met up with Stephen, who described that he had been scanning the area and had seen something tall, white and bipedal, walk between two trees. The sighting had been quick, a blink and you'll miss it, type situation. Stephen said the creature appeared to have a mohawk like mane that started on its head and down it's back. We searched the area where he had seen it but were unable to find any tracks or sign. The ground in the area where the creature was sighted was very spongy and soft.

We pushed forward through the "Valley of Death," and walked to where the open ground met with the tree line. Past the tree line the ground began to gain in elevation. We walked into the woods a little way and stopped to eat lunch.

We ate our lunch in mostly silence, listening as we ate, trying to hear anything that may be moving in the thick forest around us. The rest of our time on the ground was rather uneventful and we decided to head back to the Puk-Uk and back to the Homer Harbor.

After returning from Port Chatham, I found myself even more obsessed with all things Bigfoot. I also developed a fascination with the area of Port Chatham. I would often find myself daydreaming of building a small cabin in the area and living off the land. Our next trip into the area, would mostly cure me of any romantic notions I had about the area.

CHAPTER 14
THE 2019 PORT CHATHAM EXPEDITION

In May of 2019, Stephen, Josiah and I returned to Port Chatham. This time, Adam was able to go with us. Also, in tow, was a film crew from England. They had arranged with Stephen to go with us and do some filming for an upcoming television show. I was excited to be a part of an actual television production and was looking forward to working with them.

The Puk-Uk was unavailable for the time we wanted to go, so Stephen secured another boat called the Kingpin. The Kingpin was a smaller, but much faster boat than the Puk-Uk. Stephen and I had initially decided that we would sleep on shore and the film crew could have the bunks on the Kingpin. That plan was quickly scrapped when we saw how rough the weather was supposed to be during our time in Port Chatham.

The Kingpin had a galley and common area that had benches that could function as makeshift bunks in a pinch. The problem was, there were not enough for all of us. Being the youngest "adventurer" on the trip and being the most climatized to the Alaskan weather, I volunteered to sleep out on the deck. Luckily,

Captain Gabe had a cot stowed away somewhere, and I was able to sleep on the cot, out on the covered deck of the Kingpin.

With the Kingpin being a smaller and faster boat, we were able to make the journey from the Homer Harbor to Port Chatham in two hours, as opposed to the six-hour chug it took on the Puk-Uk. Captain Gabe liked to go fast.

Pulling into Port Chatham, we had several hours of daylight left to use, so we hit the ground running. We quickly rowed ashore in a zodiac, the outboard on the little boat was inoperable, much to the crew's dismay, and checked out an area we had not been to before. We quickly scouted around the area and placed a trail camera. There was a well-worn trail near the area we had come ashore, and believed that we would be able to capture something on camera.

During the last trip, we had done things at our own pace, Josiah had been in charge of the filming and although, a novice filmmaker, his primary goal had been to document the expedition. This one however, was a bit different. Josiah was there of course, and was continuing to document our exploits but now there was also a four-person professional film crew there as well.

During this second trip to Port Chatham, we had more goals than to just explore the area and look for the Nantiinaq, we had to film a TV show.

Most of our time on this trip was devoted to getting shots for the film crew. We spent a lot of time walking along the beach in the rain, only to be told to walk back, turn around and do it again. Somewhere, there is a hard drive with hours of footage of Stephen, Adam and I walking around in slow motion on the Port Chatham beach.

Don't get me wrong, it was a really cool experience, and one I doubt I'll have again, but as fun as it is filming a TV show, I really, really wanted to explore more and look for the Nantiinaq. Adam, who had considerably more experience in filming productions than I did, had taken me aside prior to our departure and advised me that he expected most our time would be devoted to the film crew, and not actual research. He was right.

We spent hours talking about the Nantiinaq in front of the camera, as well as walking through the rain, often over and over again in the same spot, for the camera. Very little time was spent actually looking and exploring. That being said, there were several aspects of the trip that took on a bizarre aspect and would help to cure my longing and admiration for the area.

As I had mentioned before, our initial plan was to let the film crew sleep on the boat and Stephen, Adam and I would sleep on the shore, near the old townsite. We had planned on taking turns standing watch while we each took turns sleeping. The weather had quickly put a kibosh on that plan. Almost as soon as the Kingpin had pulled into Port Chatham, the weather had turned sour.

Torrential rains, as well as strong winds dominated the area for the time we were there. It seemed as if a storm had descended into the bay and circled for almost the entire time we were there. Strangely enough, there would be breaks in the weather in which the wind would die down and the rain would lessen in intensity. We would notice these breaks in the weather and begin to gear up for another jaunt ashore for more filming.

Every time, without fail, as soon as we were geared up and ready to depart the boat, the weather would instantly increase in intensity. We began to joke that there was something that did not want us there in Port Chatham. Initially, it was said in jest. By the time we left, most of us truly believed it.

The first night after filming, we had a nice dinner prepared by Captain Gabe, then it was time for bed. I had set up my borrowed cot on the covered back deck of the Kingpin and had settled into my sleeping bag. Even though it was May, it was still getting quite dark at night and by the time we had called it a night, darkness was falling. I had placed my little cot close to the entrance of the galley, off to the side, and as far away from the stern as I could get.

I was tired from the day's activities of filming and walking through the rough terrain. I wasn't in much better shape on this trip than the previous one, but had made some improvements to my unhealthy lifestyle and had made some efforts to improve my stamina. The gentle rocking of the boat, and the patter of the rain on the canvas cover above me, was quickly lulling me to sleep.

Before I succumbed to sleep, my mind drifted to an encounter I had read in *Rain Coast Sasquatch,* it was a recounting of a young man, coming up on deck of the fishing vessel he was on, only to find a large Sasquatch crawling out of the water, onto the boat. The encounter had ended safely enough, with the Sasquatch, seeing the young man and leaping back into the water from the boat and swimming away. (Alley, 2003) Given the history of our current location and the fact that all that separated me from the outside world at the moment was a few millimeters of canvas and a waist high, fiberglass gate, even in my exhausted state, as I drifted off to sleep, I had concerns.

I awoke to a loud *CRASH* and a crushing weight pushing down on me. "Oh, my God!" I thought, "The Nantiinaq got on the boat and is trying to get me!" Those were the thoughts that raced through my head, until I realized that the Nantiinaq smelled like cigarettes and Stoli's Vodka. Groggily, I realized that Stephen had stepped out on the deck for a cigarette and had somehow tripped and landed square on top of me. After making sure we were both okay, Stephen had his smoke and made his way back inside. After that considerable, and justified, adrenaline dump, I found it much harder to fall back to sleep.

The next day, after breakfast, Captain Gabe came down from the wheelhouse and told everyone we were about to be boarded by the Alaska State Troopers. The troopers were out patrolling in their boat and had spent the night moored up not far from the Kingpin. Captain Gabe was not happy about potentially being boarded. Not because we were doing anything wrong or illegal, but because the trooper vessel did not have fenders, rubber plastic implements that are attached to the boat, like tires or buoys to absorb impact and prevent boats from rubbing on things like docks or other boats. You see, Captain Gabe kept an immaculate boat and was very particular about the condition of his vessel. Captain Gabe did not want the trooper's vessel rafting up to the Kingpin and scratching the paint.

Captain Gabe, rushed out to the deck and started conversing with the troopers on board. Personally, I was not crazy about the idea that the troopers wanted to board the Kingpin either. At that point, I was working as a police officer and my interest and activities in the Bigfoot community were not public knowledge at this point. I knew the troopers would come onboard and want to see everyone's identification and I was sure that one of the troopers would either recognize me or my name and I would soon be "outed."

Luckily, Captain Gabe was on the job. Captain Gabe began talking to the trooper on the deck of the patrol boat. The trooper told Captain Gabe that they wanted to come aboard and check everyone's hunting license.

"No one is hunting." Captain Gabe replied. "They are filming a TV show, looking for Bigfoot."

I almost wish I could have seen the look on the trooper's face when he said that. I was sitting at the galley table, listening to the exchange. Obviously, the trooper either didn't understand, or believe what Captain Gabe was telling him because the exchange that followed could only be compared to the "Who's on first?" routine that Abbott and Costello made famous.

Trooper, "We just want to come and check everyone's hunting license."

Captain Gabe, "No one has a license, they aren't hunting, they are looking for Bigfoot and filming a TV show.

Trooper, "We want to check their hunting licenses."

Captain Gabe, "They aren't hunting…they are filming a show on Bigfoot. They don't have hunting licenses."

Trooper, "We want to board and check their hunting licenses."

Captain Gabe, "Okay...that's fine...but no one has a license, it's a film crew from England and some Bigfoot researchers. None of them have hunting licenses."

Trooper, "Oh."

The Trooper then told Captain Gabe they would leave us alone and to have a good day. They then puttered off on their way, I'm sure having quite the interesting conversation about the exchange that had just occurred. I breathed a sigh of relief, knowing my secret was safe for another day.

We observed a break in the weather and began to gear up. Almost like clockwork, as we piled into the little zodiac, the wind began to pick up and the rain began to come down even harder. The outboard motor that had been attached to the zodiac was dead upon our arrival at Port Chatham, even though Captain Gabe and his first mate had tested it prior to our departure. More bad luck, or more sinister complications?

First Mate Jimmy got the arduous task of rowing us ashore. Between the rain and the winds, rowing the zodiac was no small task. Several times, on our short excursions in the zodiac, the little boat would be pushed around in the rough seas, to the point I seriously became concerned for our well-being. Even though we were not far from the Kingpin, or shore, I believe if we had got dunked in the cold Alaskan waters, chances were good, some of us, would not make it out of the frigid water. Especially not since I had a heavy shotgun strapped across my chest.

I guided the film crew up to the area where the derelict equipment lay, it appeared just as it had a few months before when we were there. There seemed to be less physical activity there this trip. At one point, Josiah pranked the film crew by donning a Bigfoot costume and trying to scare them. I was quite amused when the director told me he thought it was a deer!

Whether it was the time of year, or the inclement weather, or perhaps even the size of our group, we were sorely disappointed with Port Chatham this time around. There was one peculiar day however, that sticks out in my mind.

We had settled into the red roofed structure near the shore and were setting up for interviews with the film crew. Stephen and Adam filmed their segments first. While they were filming, I had to be very quiet but wanted to remain in the small cabin to stay out of the rain. I took a post at the rear of the cabin, facing into the wood line. There were no doors or windows in the cabin, just holes where they used to be.

I passed the time by staring out the back of the little cabin, looking for sign of bear, the Nantiinaq or anything else that could be lurking in the woods. At one point, I observed what I took to be a translucent shimmering in a nearby pine tree, it was very high up, probably ten feet or more and it was just the briefest shimmer of movement. The branches moved beneath it as if it was putting weight on them and shook for a few seconds after it disappeared. The whole event lasted all of three to four seconds.

Full disclosure, it was raining at the time I observed this, and I took it to be a collection of rain that had pooled somewhere higher up on the tree and either by weight or breeze, had been dislodged, striking the branches on the way down. While I had certainly heard stories of encounters with a shimmering translucent figure, much like the creature from the *Predator* movies. The shape I saw was neither humanoid or appeared to move in any direction other than down like it was dropping or falling. I watched the area for a few minutes and observed nothing else out of the ordinary and soon dismissed it as just falling rainwater. I told no one about the strange sight.

The rest of my time looking out the back of the little cabin was uneventful and soon enough, it was my turn to sit in front of the camera and talk about Port Chatham. It was now Adam and Stephen's turn to sit in the back of the cabin and be quiet.

During my interview, which lasted some time, Stephen alerted us that he had heard something outside in the rear of the cabin. At one point, Stephen racked a round into his shotgun and said sternly, "Something is fuckin' out there." Later, Stephen would explain he saw and heard branches shake and heard something growl. I did not hear or see what Stephen had heard, but the described activity was taking place very much near where I had observed the strange distortion in the tree earlier.

I completed my interview and while the film crew collected their items, Adam, Stephen and I poked around the back of the cabin. We did not go into the wood line.

That night I was looking forward to crawling into my sleeping bag and getting some rest. After the previous night's "attack" I was looking forward to some restful sleep. That was not to be the case. I was awoken to a loud boom and the boat was shaking, vibrating. I rose up from my cot and looked around. I didn't hear or see anything amiss. I heard Captain Gabe stirring in the wheelhouse. I could hear the others talking inside the boat and heard the word "earthquake" used. I had lived in Alaska long enough to be familiar with earthquakes but had never been on a boat during one.

The next morning, my wife texted me via my satellite communication device and asked if we'd felt the earthquake. I confirmed we had, and that she had confirmed to us that it had been an earthquake. I told Captain Gabe and we spent several moments arguing over whether you could feel an earthquake in a boat or not. Captain Gabe insisted that we should not have been able to feel an earthquake in the boat. I countered that since we were in a bay, and the ground was moving on either side of us, that it would undoubtably ripple into the bay and we would feel it. We left the argument in a stalemate with neither budging on our respective positions. I could not understand what we felt the previous night, if we could not feel earthquakes, according to Captain Gabe.

After some final filming on the shore, the film crew rendezvoused with another boat and headed back to civilization. Adam, Stephen and I had another day to explore and look around. Without the presence of the film crew, we were able to devote more time to exploring and looking around. We went back to the area nicknamed the "Valley of Death" by Stephen.

Adam likes to find an area in which animals may congregate, like watering holes or food sources, and sit and wait. He has had success with this method in the past and it is his go-to method while out in the field. We did this for a while without results near the "Valley of Death."

I checked out the area where I found the fourteen-inch track from the last trip and found no new impressions. Our short foray into the "Valley of Death" was about the only time during this trip that it did not rain.

Just like that, our time in Port Chatham was again over, even though it did not seem to be as active as the last time we were there, the weather and the seas made it no less hair-raising. Stephen and I were both sure we were going to get tossed out of the tiny zodiac and I have no doubt that on one occasion, if my ample backside had not been weighing down the bow, the little boat would have likely been flipped in the rough waters.

Unlike the first time I left Port Chatham, this time, I did not leave yearning to go back. Long after our first trip in, I had fantasized about building a cabin somewhere in the area and spending time living off the land and searching for the Nantiinaq. Upon leaving this second time, I was thankful to get out of there alive. Between the gruesome weather and strange, invisible growling entities, I felt that somehow, Port Chatham had enough of our presence and was not so politely, showing us the door.

I think it's important to mention that after this trip, Stephen reported that he had been plagued with terrible nightmares about Port Chatham. Beastly creatures came after him in his dreams and left him with a healthy respect and fear of the area. We have briefly pondered a return trip to the area but a mix of logistics and dread have seemed to thwart us at every turn. Maybe someday we will return.

The beach at Port Chatham.

Photo credit: Extreme Expeditions Northwest, LLC, 2018 Port Chatham Expedition

Photo of the mysterious trash pile.

Photo credit: Larry Baxter, 2018 Port Chatham Expedition

One of the abandoned structures at Port Chatham.
Photo credit: Extreme Expeditions Northwest, LLC, 2018 Port Chatham Expedition

Machinery left at Port Chatham.

Photo credit: Extreme Expeditions Northwest, LLC, 2018 Port Chatham Expedition

Track found size 10.5 boot for scale.
Photo credit: Larry Baxter, 2018 Port Chatham Expedition

From left to right.
Larry "Beans" Baxter, Stephen Major, Adam Davies ready to depart Port Chatham after the 2019 Port Chatham Expedition.
Photo credit, Josiah Martin

CHAPTER 15
LIVING HISTORY

After my second trip to Port Chatham, my desire to return to the area certainly took a decline. At one point, I was approached by a group who wanted to go into the area on an expedition and had actually wanted to try and land a small plane in the field next to the red-roofed cabin. The one that was littered with logs! I have to admit, I felt much like Jeff Goldblum's character in *The Lost World: Jurassic Park,* trying to convince them that they would likely die if they attempted such a feat. I believe my advice to them was basically, "Don't go."

Even though my desire to return to Port Chatham had waned, I still found myself fascinated with the area. At first glance, there is no place like it on Earth. Many ghost towns are found across the landscape of North America. However, most conventional ghost towns follow a familiar formula. Resources such as gold, silver or some such other valuable item is found to be in abundance in the area, and a town is established. People and industry move into the area to either make a living with the nearby resources, or to make a living supplying those who are working with the resources. Then things "boom" for the town and a halcyon period is experienced while the resources and fruits of labor are enjoyed.

However, all good things must, eventually, end. Mines are played out, forests are logged out, animals are trapped, fished are hunted to near extinction levels, and life becomes harder for the people in the town. People will then begin to move away, to seek fortunes or just an easier life, somewhere else. Eventually, with the resources depleted, you will have your classic ghost town, standing alone and abandoned.

Port Chatham seemingly did not follow this formula. The retellings of the abandonment of Port Chatham portray a town that was abandoned almost overnight, still rich with resources and opportunity. Modern news articles and internet retellings of the history of Port Chatham will often conjure up images of the fearful residents, running for their lives, glancing over their shoulders to the dark wood line, as they rush toward waiting boats to escape unseen horrors in the woods.

I was hungry for more information on Port Chatham. I was fascinated with the idea of how such a resource rich area could be abandoned. I took off my adventurer hat and put on my detective hat. I was determined to learn more about the history of Port Chatham. Luckily, I lived in the right area to make that happen.

As I have stated previously, many stories regarding Port Chatham are lost to time. People who lived and worked in the area are reaching an advanced age and we are beginning to lose the living history of the area at an alarming rate. The legends and lore that reside on the internet is forever, but the actual living history of the area is dying out. I was fortunate during my investigation to be able to speak to someone who was born in Port Chatham and grew up there. Living, speaking, history.

Joseph "Joe" Carlough was born in Port Chatham in 1933. Joe would have been 17 years old in 1950, when the town was abandoned. If anyone was in the know regarding the history of Port Chatham, it would be Joe.

One of the first things I wanted to clarify with Joe was the confusion about the two towns, Portlock and Port Chatham. Regarding this Joe said, "There was just the town as you came in on the right-hand side of the bay (where the red roofed structure is) and across the bay, by the lagoon, there were some houses there, where people lived."

According to Joe, it was just the main town of Portlock where the main concentration of buildings and residences were, and there was no official separate town of Port Chatham. Port Chatham is the name of the bay.

Joe explained a bit about everyday life in Port Chatham, there were no vehicles and everyone walked to where they needed to be or took a boat. "It was just a little native village." He mused. Around 50 people lived in the town and lived there year-round. There was no doctor in the tiny village and if you needed medical help you had to go to Seldovia, or farther, for treatment.

Joe said that the town did not have electricity but the cannery had its own powerplant or generator. There was running water in the town Joe confirmed. I had remembered seeing old pipes in the ground, near the townsite, during my two trips there.

In describing the town, Joe said there was a smokehouse, the cannery, a school and even a "pretty good-sized mink farm." Surprisingly, Joe described the sawmill and not the cannery as the economic driving force of the tiny town. "The sawmill that done all the capping for the traps (fish traps) and stuff." Joe explained.

When asked about the legends surrounding Port Chatham and the stories of Nantiinaq and the Bigfoot, Joe laughed, "Yeah, there were always stories about it and people coming around looking for Bigfoot. I never saw him."

Joe's dismissal of the Bigfoot legends made me even more curious about the reason the town was left abandoned. I sat, glued to the conversation, completely focused on the words that Joe spoke. Not only was I getting firsthand information from someone who was born and raised in Port Chatham, I was getting answers to questions that likely, few outside local native communities and villages had heard or had even bothered to seek out.

Joe's testimonial continued, "Yeah, everybody left 'cause it just died off. There was the big sawmill there, that was the main part of Port Chatham, they made the capping for all the fish traps and then that burned up and that pretty much…settled that."

I asked Joe, "So Bigfoot didn't chase everybody out?"

Joe laughed, "No, he didn't bother me any!"

Having heard that, I decided to ask Joe about the mysterious deaths attributed to Port Chatham.

"Did you ever hear about the mysterious or suspicious deaths in Port Chatham?" I asked.

Joe replied, "No, no, there are a lot of rumors going around about Port Chatham, I think they're wrong, bogus."

Joe explained, "The Nelson family owned the smokehouse, the cannery and the sawmill, they took care of pretty much everything." Joe went on to explain that the same family had also owned or purchased a smokehouse in Bellingham, Washington and that when they had moved on, pretty much everyone else had left too.

Joe said the sawmill had caught fire, it was a big sawmill and that the sawmill had made all the lumber for the salmon traps that were in the inlet.

Joe imparted that the loss of the sawmill in the fire, along with government restrictions on the salmon traps, had led the owners of the businesses in Port Chatham to leave the area.

"It killed everything." Joes said. The absence of the town's economic pillars, slowly led to the town being a less accommodating place to live. With almost no businesses to support a working family, most left soon after the fire, for more accommodating pastures, such as Seldovia.

"It was just a little village, when I was there and then everyone moved out, so there was nothing left." Joe said. "It wasn't scary at all, just a little village." Joe laughed.

After my conversation with Joe, I began to look at Port Chatham in a different light. Perhaps the timeline of Port Chatham **did** fit the profile of so many other ghost towns. Unlike other ghost towns however, instead of losing the resources, the town lost the means to process and refine the resources.

Friend and fellow researcher, Jessie Desmond, brought a newspaper article she found to my attention. According to an article published in the Fairbanks Daily News Miner, February 1938, a fire destroyed the sawmill, the cannery and other buildings in Portlock. The fire was reported to have started from a blacksmith's forge and none of the buildings were insured. (Buildings at Portlock Go Up in Smoke, 1938)

Between the conversation and the article, I was convinced that Bigfoot, or Nantiinaq did not chase everyone out of the town. Port Chatham, like so many other ghost towns before it, fell victim to the one monster that plagues us all, money. Rather than rebuild, the owners, who owned both the sawmill and the cannery, decided to cut their losses and leave. Perhaps they knew that eventually, the fish traps that supplied the majority of their product would eventually be banned. Fish traps were banned in 1959, striking quite a blow to the fishing industry at the time. Often, such legislation can be years in the making, and perhaps, it was being talked about as early as 1938. Hearing such damaging legislation was on the table it may have influenced any business owner who just suffered a catastrophic loss to rethink their position and move on.

Whether it was the fire, the cost of rebuilding, the talk of crippling legislation or a combination of all those factors and more, we may never know. My curiosity surrounding the abandonment of Port Chatham satisfied, I found even more evidence contrary to the legends surrounding the little bay.

Not only is Port Chatham described as the town where all the residents were chased out by Bigfoot, it also has another stigma attached to it as an "evil place" and a place where the natives refuse to go and avoid at all cost. Once again, I found evidence to refute this. I found evidence that there was a native settlement in Port Chatham. A village called Axu `layik was located at Port Chatham. I have no information as to the size, population or even if it was a year-round settlement or not, but the very existence of a native settlement in Port Chatham seems to negate many of the "evil place" legends that surround the area. Of course, one could make the claim that the settlement of the village was how they determined the place was evil.

CHAPTER 16
THE LEGEND LIVES

Perhaps I still have some of that young boy from Kentucky who devoured library monster books inside me? Even after hearing Joe's logical explanation as to why Port Chatham was abandoned, even knowing that it wasn't quite the evil, malevolent place it is often portrayed as in news and internet stories, I *still believe* in Port Chatham.

I doubt that a fire, even an economy crippling one, such as the one that occurred in 1938, could result in the formation of such a fearful symmetry of legend. Even with the aspects of the legend surrounding it debunked, Port Chatham still has mysteries. I know that my fellow expedition members saw and heard things they cannot explain. I cannot deny the thermal footage I myself captured or the 14-inch track I found. I do believe, there is more to Port Chatham than meets the eye.

Just because Port Chatham wasn't abandoned because of unknown upright, hairy, beings, does not mean they do not exist. An area with a healthy history of sightings could easily garner the reputation that it was abandoned because of the unconventional encounters that occurred there. Between the years and generations, tales of sightings, fires and economic collapse, could morph into a tale of frightening escape.

In fact, for those with a predilection toward the supernatural and Fortean, the revelation of the economy destroying fire, may only feed the macabre and unearthly aspects of the history of Port Chatham. Future retellings of the legend of Port Chatham may include fearful residents fleeing an all-engulfing fire as it consumes the town. Stealing glances over their shoulders as they run for the boats, they hear the howls of the Nantiinaq as it reclaims its land.

What of the Nantiinaq? The legendary beast man was around before the abandonment of Port Chatham and continues to walk his way into more modern settings and sightings. Even today, fishermen who anchor their boats in Port Chatham to escape storms or rough seas will whisper among themselves tales of tall, black shadows they see walking around the coastline. Is it the elusive one-eyed people? The ghostly Dark Lady? The lost souls of hunters and prospectors who never made it out of the wilderness? Or the Nantiinaq, keeping watch over the intruding ships?

We may never know if any of the hidden, cryptid denizens of Port Chatham exist physically, in imagination, or some other, intangible or interdimensional form. But, one thing is for certain, the trepidation and fear they inspire is very real.

CHAPTER 17
MORE SIGHTINGS ON THE KENAI PENINSULA

Tales of upright, hairy bipedal creatures are not exclusive to Port Chatham and have been reported all over the state, including a healthy concentration on the rest of the Kenai Peninsula. The following sightings are a mixture of those I have collected from other Alaska based researchers and some that were reported to, and experienced by, me directly:

- 1974, sighting, tracks and vocals involving lost snowmachiners ~ sasquatchtracker.com

- 1977, tracks discovered in a deep ravine. ~sasquatchtracker.com

- 1980's, Skilak Lake Road, a hunter describes seeing a 6 to 7ft. tall hairy man walk across the road. The figure stopped, looked at him and continued across the road. The man loaded his shotgun and promptly left the area. ~bfro.net and sasquatchtracker.com

- 1998, Skilak Lake Road, sighting on dirt road near Skilak Lake. ~sasquatchtracker.com

- 2004, husband and wife traveling south on the Sterling Highway near Sterling, AK see a large bipedal figure run across the road. They slowed down near the area where it crossed and looked but saw nothing else. ~Reported to Author, 2018

- 2015, Skilak Lake Road, a firefighter engaged in firefighting operations briefly observed a tall bipedal animal walking into the woods. No other crews were working in the area and the firefighter cited upright posture and extremities proportions and did not believe it to be a bear. ~sasquatchtracker.com

- 2016, Moose Pass, AK a hiker discovers tracks near Upper Trail Lake. Hiker described a 16.5-inch left foot print near the shoreline of the lake. Other less discernable tracks were observed in the water. Tracks were estimated to be 5 to 6ft. apart. ~sasquatchtracker.com

- 2017, Bottenintnin Lake, large human foot like imprint found in the ground, later, in the same area, loud ground-shaking thumping heard with no explainable origin. ~sasquatchtracker.com and Author's personal experience.

- 2018, near Summit Lake, AK truck driver reports two separate sightings of a large bipedal creature walking near his truck while parked at a pull-out at night. ~sasquatchtracker.com

- 2019, Rainbow Lake, a woman kayaking with her husband come around a bend in the lake and observe a large dark bipedal figure that they first believed to be a man. The figure grabbed two large pine trees by the trunks and began shaking them very forcefully, then walked into the thick brush. The kayakers later returned to the area, via kayak, and attempted to re-create the event. The husband who was 5'11" was swallowed up by the thick terrain and vegetation. The figure they had seen was much larger than the husband. I attempted to hike into the location of the sighting and found the area to be impossible to reach on foot in summer. The brush and terrain are unbelievably thick. Sighting reported to Author in 2020.

CHAPTER 18
THEORIES AND CONCLUSIONS

The number of theories as to what the phenomenon of Bigfoot or Sasquatch is, almost rivals the number of sightings of the creature itself. From shape-shifting, trans dimensional aliens, to undiscovered ape species, the theories run the gamut from those based on logic and reasoning to ideas that would make the most imaginative science-fiction writer shake their head.

Based on the number of sightings, just in the United States alone, one would be foolish to dismiss the phenomenon outright. People are seeing *something!* Undoubtably some sightings are misidentifications of existing animals; some are hoaxes, while still others are no doubt products of delusional minds. However, it only takes one legitimate, true sighting, for the phenomenon to be real.

Personally, as of right now, I believe the phenomenon has a very physical component. I know many start out firmly entrenched in the physical camp and eventually end up turning to more metaphysical explanations. I'm sure after years of near misses and close calls, many enthusiasts seek solace in the explanation that there is a supernatural element to the phenomenon that is keeping them from the answers they seek.

I know there are things in this world that are, at this point, unexplainable. However, things that were once considered magic and otherworldly, now have rational scientific explanations. When humans do not understand something, we tend to make up stories to explain the phenomenon, like gods being responsible for thunder and lighting. Eventually, knowledge is unlocked that takes the gods out of the equation and makes the thunder and lightning, rational events found in nature.

For every sighting of Bigfoot out there in which he is reported to display strange, otherworldly abilities, there are sightings in which they are observed displaying behavior that parallels with that of great apes. Is it that great a leap in logic to believe there could be something out there between ape and man? Some offshoot of the evolutionary tree that is yet to be cataloged?

When approached with questions about the existence of Bigfoot, most academics and scientists will bring out the stock answer saying that there are not enough calories in the woods to keep such an animal alive. I have two major problems with that answer. The first, there are certainly animals of that size in the woods right now. Bears and moose are found in many forests of the world, somehow, they manage to keep themselves fed and live through some very rough winters. Second, that is a very bold assertion considering you know nothing of how the metabolism of such a creature may have evolved. Nature is certainly amazing and efficient and often finds ways of thriving that can seem almost magical to the casual observer. For every argument against their existence, a logical counter-argument can be made. Entire books have been written addressing almost all of these arguments and more.

We as a society have become very accustomed to being told what to think and believe. All it takes is for a person with an official title or few initials after their name to be quoted in an article or to make an appearance on the news and that is the final word on things. We have confused formal education with experience and knowledge. Those with little or no experience are being led by those whose most adverse moments in their lives, consist of turning in homework assignments on time.

There are a few scientists and academics out there who do hold an interest in the phenomenon. Generally, those most interested are the ones that have spent actual time out in the field studying and searching for specific target species. It would seem, the ones with the most field experience, are the ones with the most interest.

Unfortunately, they are forced to keep their interest in the subject secret, unable to voice their theories and ideas on the subject in fear of ridicule or even professional black listing.

Being a former law enforcement professional, I can certainly relate to their desire to keep their interest out of the prying eyes of others. It is demoralizing to be called crazy and delusional by people you work with and respect, just for having an open mind. Just imagine, in a world where new species are being discovered all the time; new species of deer, ape and even whales are being discovered well into the 21st century and you are getting called insane because you believe in the *possibility* of an undiscovered primate! If you are not crazy when you develop an interest in Bigfoot, you will be after dealing with the uninitiated soon enough.

The sad truth of the matter is, until there is money available for research and study, the scientific community will continue to ignore the phenomenon. Much like the fire charred economy of Port Chatham, the Bigfoot phenomenon finds itself at the mercy of the biggest beast of all: money.

Ultimately, the burden of proof lies upon us, the enthusiasts, the citizen scientists and those who hold a burning desire to solve a mystery hundreds of years old. Whether your idea of research is looking up old stories on the internet, camping in active areas or bushwhacking into abandoned Alaskan ghost towns, no contribution, no matter how minor, should be discounted.

No doubt, I'll gear up again, strap on my bear spray and shotgun and wander into the woods again in search of answers. I started my journey looking for answers. I've found few. What I have found over the years however, are new friends, adventures and memories that made every cold, wet, muscle burning moment worth it. I can't wait to do it again.

SPECIAL ACKNOWLEDGMENTS

This book would not exist without my very special friends Adam Davies and Stephen Major. Thank you both for introducing me to a world of adventure, excitement and danger. Thank you to Josiah Martin of Martin Media for being there with your camera every step of the way. Very special thank you to Joe Carlough for sharing his story with me and to all the people I spoke to about the history of Port Chatham. Special thanks to Extreme Expeditions Northwest, LLC for the cover photo, provided from the 2018 Port Chatham Expedition. A very special thank you to the English Bay Corporation for allowing us access to your land, it was an amazing experience.

REFERENCES

Alley, J. R. (2003). *Raincoast Sasquatch*. Blaine, WA: Hancock House.

Bragg, B. (2015, June 23). Hunters bag 2 huge brown bears on Kenai Peninsula. *Anchorage Daily News*.

Buildings at Portlock Go Up in Smoke. (1938, February 16). *Fairbanks Daily News Miner*, p. 7.

Colm A. Kelleher, P. a. (2005). *Hunt for the Skinwalker*. New York: Pocket Books.

Evans, V. (1980). Searching For Roots at Portlock. *Alexandrovsk No. 1*, pp. 42-47.

Kalifornsky, P. (1991). *A Dena'ina Legacy: K'tl'egh'i Sukdu: The Collected Writings of Peter Kalifornsky 1st Edition*. Alaska Native Language Center.

Kehl, M. (2014, December 18). *Youtube*. Retrieved from Kathy Brewster and Malania Kehl: Story of Bigfoot : https://www.youtube.com/watch?v=oD2mp0I_las

Klouda, N. (2009, October 28). Haunting memories — 'Nantiinaq' sightings, spirits led to desertion of Native village. *Homer Tribune*.

Martin, J. (Director). (2019). *In Search of the Port Chatham Hairy Man* [Motion Picture].

Pulu, F. S. (1979). *Old Beliefs*. National Bilingual Materials Development Center Rural Education.

Made in the USA
Las Vegas, NV
29 March 2022

46523953R00085